Rediscovering
the Integral Cosmos

Physics, Metaphysics, and Vertical Causality

Jean Borella *&* Wolfgang Smith

Rediscovering
the
Integral Cosmos

*Physics, Metaphysics,
and Vertical Causality*

Introduction by
Bruno Bérard

 Angelico Press

Originally published in France as
Physique et métaphysique
Collection Métaphysique au quotidien
Copyright © L'Harmattan, 2018
www.harmattan.fr

First published in English by Angelico Press, 2018
Copyright © Angelico Press 2018

For information, address:
Angelico Press
169 Monitor St.
Brooklyn, NY 11222
www.angelicopress.com

978-1-62138-407-6 (pbk)
978-1-62138-408-3 (cloth)
978-1-62138-409-0 (ebook)

Cover design: Michael Schrauzer

CONTENTS

PART II: IS SCIENCE THROUGH WITH GOD?:
A PHILOSOPHICAL ESSAY
by *Jean Borella*

Introduction

The great metaphysicians of every epoch are often mathematicians or physicists also—or have at least studied these disciplines. Such was the case with Pythagoras, as also with Plato, the great mathematician of the *Timaeus*, who—tradition tells us—had engraved over the entrance to the Academy: "Let no one enter here unless he be a geometer."[1] Such was also the case with Descartes, Pascal, Leibniz, and Hegel,[2] and, more recently, with Whitehead, Guénon, and Heidegger.[3] It will come as no surprise, then, that Jean Borella, professor of philosophy and metaphysics, also earned a degree in physics during his studies.

On the other hand physicists, mathematicians, and even logicians are much less often philosophers—and even more rarely metaphysicians. This is nevertheless the case, of course, with Aristotle, and in a certain way with Husserl[4] or more recently with René Thom, David Chalmers,[5] or Robert Bolton, for example. And so Wolfgang Smith's situation is quite rare: for here is a professor of mathematics and physics (most notably at MIT[6] and UCLA[7]) who became a metaphysician.

1. The importance of geometry in the formation of the philosopher can be read in *Republic* VII, 526c8–527c11 (development of the capacity of abstraction for access to the intelligible), and is illustrated by the experience of the slave of Meno (*Meno* 80d1–86d2).

2. Hegel studied physics and mathematics at the Tübingen seminary (1788–1789).

3. Heidegger studied mathematics, physics and chemistry at the Faculty of Natural Sciences of the University of Friborg (1911–1912). His criticism of metaphysics (refutable and refuted) does not make him any less of a metaphysician.

4. Husserl first studied mathematics with the great mathematician Karl Weierstrass.

5. Chalmers' initial studies focused on mathematics at the University of Adelaide.

6. Massachusetts Institute of Technology (Cambridge, USA).

7. University of California, Los Angeles (Los Angeles).

When a metaphysician has some skill in physics, or more generally in the (exact) sciences, or a scientist has some expertise in metaphysics, we are already assured of a discourse that gives the "natural
world" a part to play—for physics comes first, then metaphysics follows, for any who seek to see further, or beyond. Thus, the founder
of science, Aristotle—whatever his misunderstanding of his
teacher's doctrine of the Ideas (Plato was his teacher for nineteen
years) may have been—followed his physics with his metaphysics,
to which the former necessarily refers.[8]

For example, the scientific question of the finitude or infinitude
of the universe seems to point only to the descriptive theories concerning this.[9] But actually, "whether space be infinite or not, only a
finite and computable volume is accessible to observation. The
background radiation of the sky marks a horizon, an ultimate wall
that all observation will forever come up against. For in its primordial phase, the universe yields up nothing to our sight: neither light
nor stars nor any other starry body were formed as yet!"[10]

Is this not why all cosmology can only be "a probable myth" (*ton
eikota mython*)?[11] Or as the astrophysicist James Jeans (1877–1946)
more recently said: "The universe begins to look more like a great
thought than like a great machine."[12]

8. It is argued that this arrangement (fixed by the publisher of Aristotle's works)
only endowed "meta" with its meaning of "after," but the publisher could have just
as well intended or included another of its meanings: "meta-" ("beyond") physical,
which, moreover, becomes clear upon reading the Philosopher.

9. This question arises, indeed, only scientifically; metaphysically, the cause is
understood. In short, neither the beginning nor the end of space is part of it, by
definition, just as the beginning and end of time are not part of time. What limits
one thing is of a different nature: the sea does not limit the sea.

10. Jean-Pierre Luminet, "L'univers est-il chiffonné?," http://luth2.obspm.fr/
~luminet /topo.html.

11. Plato, *Timaeus*, 29d.

12. *The Mysterious Universe* (Cambridge: Cambridge University Press, 1930),
137. Thus, for the astrophysicist Christian Magnan (1942), an infinite universe is
simply a useless, even perverse, hypothesis. Because the principle of a homogeneous
and isotopic universe (even on a large scale) is not demonstrated, and because "an
infinite mathematical model cannot be related, technically, to the real, and this situation is completely contrary to the scientific approach. . . . Science cannot support

In any case, this is why it seemed essential to bring together in this book both approaches: that of physicist and mathematician Wolfgang Smith, led to think through the understanding of these disciplines as a metaphysician; and that of metaphysician Jean Borella, who considers the world and man with the necessary hindsight imposed by the postulates of certain strands of modern scientific thought.

Thus we have here not so much a thinking about science as such, which many have done in the past (for example, in the modern era: Fichte, Comte, Poincaré, Mach, Russell, Quine, Popper, Lakatos, Kuhn, Duhem, Bachelard, Piajet, Granger, Sosa, Greco, Kvanvig, Zagzebski, and many others), but a thinking about the world and man despite (or beyond) the limits of science—limits that are of two kinds. Indeed, there are the limits legitimately inherent to every discipline—since this involves their necessarily circumscribed material or formal objects[13]—but there are also ideological or cultural limits that are more insidious, and that only the rigor of philosophical thought can detect and denounce.

And so to pass these limits is simply to enter into philosophy, whether as a scientist practicing it or a philosopher engaged in it. That is why we cannot say, as does Stephen Hawking (1942–2018), that "philosophy is dead [because] it has not kept up with modern developments in science,"[14] or, like Willard Van Orman Quine (1908–2000), paragon of an exaggerated positivism, that "there should be no difference of nature between science and philosophy."[15] Such statements as these miss the formal object of philo-

a theory that escapes in advance and by nature any connection with reality"; cf. Magnan, "The infinity of cosmologists: reality or imposture?," http://www.lac osmo.com/infini-encore.html.

13. Two sciences can deal with the same material object, for example plants, but differ greatly in their very distinct formal objects: botany and pharmacology, for example.

14. Stephen Hawking and Leonard Mlodinow, *The Grand Design* (New York: Random House, 2011), 5.

15. Joseph Vidal-Rosset, *Qu'est-ce qu'un paradoxe?* (Paris: Vrin, 2004), 11. Cf. W.V.O. Quine, *Ontological Relativity and Other Essays* (New York and London: Columbia University Press, 1969), 82–84, in his "Epistemology Naturalized" lecture (ibid., 69–90).

sophy, established once and for all: "this [philosophy] is the only independent science, since it alone exists for itself."[16]

Both Borella and Smith will therefore express themselves as philosophers. And although one will speak of what eludes "horizontal sequence" (Borella) while the other articulates "vertical causality" (Smith), this is owing to the fact that we cannot escape the "metaphysical cross"—be it in cosmogony, quanta, or man. Thus, in terms of cosmogony, the doctrine of *creatio ex nihilo* (which has nothing to do with creationism) proves to be the only possible understanding of the world (Borella). But then, commencing with the incomprehensibility of quantum theory,[17] the "simple" ontological distinction between the corporeal and the physical, and the passage from potency to act (a "cosmogenetic act"), we are offered here an intelligible account of this (Smith). And so it comes as no surprise that both authors are led to recall the epistemological key that constitutes the realism of the substantial form and the notion of *materia prima*. As for man, it is easily shown (by its absurdity) that when La Mettrie (1709–1751), Laplace (1749–1827), or Hawking assert that thought is only the result of the absolute determinism of *Man a machine*,[18] their speech has no more meaning than a contrary, equally determined, discourse arising from another "machine"; therefore, speech no longer makes sense (Borella).

Both Borella and Smith also, contrary to any biopsychic idealism or "retinal reduction," are led to show vision as access to the real (existential) world and to what supports it. One concludes, following the psychologist James J. Gibson (1904–1979),[19] that this is a "vertical act" (Smith), while the other, following the philosopher Raymond Ruyer (1902–1987), and as exemplified by the evolution of pictorial art, explains the unease of the modern painter who, in the

---

16. Aristotle, *Metaphysics*, I, II, 11, trans. H. Tredennick (Cambridge, MA: Harvard University Press, 1933), 15.

17. "No one understands quantum theory," said the "great explainer" that was the physicist Richard Feynman (1918–1988).

18. See La Mettrie, *L'Homme machine* (Leiden: Luzac, 1748).

19. *The Ecological Approach to Visual Perception* (Boston: Houghton Mifflin, 1979).

4

face of the visible reality of a desacralized world, can no longer account for the invisible unless he deconstructs the world (Borella).

Similarly, both are led to show free will as irreducible: one, Smith, in connection with William Dembski's 1998 mathematical demonstration;[20] the other, Borella, as already mentioned, in connection with the absurd absolute determinism of a La Mettrie, Laplace, or Hawking.

And quite clearly, both authors lead us to realize what is outside time: Borella on the topic of form's spiritual nature (in the face of the other two natures, i.e., the corporeal and the psychic) in that it is "essentialist and actualist"; and Smith, in showing how Gibson's subtle but rigorous argument refers to Plato and a human soul that is not confined to the temporal but has access to eternity.

Whether we follow the one or the other we return to a Weltanschauung that can finally account for the world in all its dimensions, and, especially, find its meaning, a meaning weakened by several centuries of mechanical determinism, scientism—the positing of (experimental) science as sole source of knowledge—or even "scientificism" if you will, taken as designating a dogmatically atheistic scientistic materialism. Both authors counter scientifically or philosophically based arguments: Borella offers an explanation for the genesis of this reductive movement while summarizing in broad strokes the genesis of quantum physics; Smith draws a striking and enlightening portrait, accessible to all, of this physics.

A note in passing. Faced with "Cartesian *bifurcationism*,"[21] rightly denounced by Wolfgang Smith, and following Alfred North Whitehead (1861–1947), perhaps it should be suggested that Descartes was no more Cartesian than Aristotle was Aristotelian, and that in this case the "third" Cartesian substance should not be hidden from view: for Descartes, just like St. Anselm, *shows* [*montre*] (and not so

20. *The Design Inference* (Cambridge: Cambridge University Press, 1998). No physical process, be it deterministic, random, or stochastic, can produce "complex specified information" (CSI).

21. Faced with the mutual exclusion of the thinking thing and the extended thing (*res cogitans, res extensa*), one is condemned to choose—to bifurcate—in accordance with the case.

much *demonstrates* [*démontre*]) how anyone might have an experience of God, and how, far from constituting an "ontological proof" (according to Kant's reductive designation), it is more a test—but a test so "natural" and so easy to pass that one may be unaware of it. Borella will recall it here: "The 'God' meaning lives in every man," even though "knowledge of God is an unknowing" (see below).

If the question of God arises, this is because a century after Galileo (1564–1642), and despite his (now out-of-date) "empty space,"[22] in the groundwork for his hypothesis on gravitation, Newton (1643–1727) still speaks of the *sensorium Dei* (God's omnipresence to the world); whereas a century later Laplace (1749–1827) speaks of dispensing with the God hypothesis. This may have seemed compelling at the time, but in the twenty-first century a great scientist like Stephen Hawking thinks it necessary to return to it, not to demonstrate God's non-existence (non-existence is scientifically unprovable) but to confirm the uselessness of such an hypothesis.

In basic psychology, this obsession with God means that He remains irreducibly the reference, the point of view, or the anchoring for all thought, even when called superfluous or dead. Moreover, "if we are surprised, shocked, or amused when we read that God is dead, this is quite precisely because we spontaneously think that the concept of God contains existence."[23] Was not this, in a way, the meaning of the Nietzschean provocation?[24]

Still, it was necessary for philosophy to try to explain how and why science became atheistic; and this is just what Jean Borella has undertaken here—hence the title of his contribution: "Is science

---

22. Galileo was a great scholar and a good Catholic, but had two defects: his religious dogmatism, which made him wish that "the propositions, taught, but not necessarily demonstrated, [be] judged as undoubtedly false as soon as there is something contrary to Scripture!" (Letter to Christine de Lorraine, quoted in Emile Namer, *L'affaire Galilée* [Paris: Gallimard & Julliard, 1975], 113); his physics, which made "the essence of the bodily substance . . . the extension," space being no more than a "purely neutral container," a "cosmic corpse" (cf. Jean Borella, *The Crisis of Religious Symbolism*, trans. G. John Champoux [Kettering, OH: Angelico Press, 2016], 80–85).

23. Thibault Gress, *Descartes et la précarité du monde* (Paris: CNRS, 2012).

24. See *The Gay Science*, Book III, 125.

through with God?" And of course Smith's "vertical causality," which makes its appearance everywhere in physics, explicitly refers to God; hence his contribution: "Physics and Vertical Causation."

Physics is first, then comes metaphysics, we said. This is what has led to the order of this book, even though, as will be seen, both sections deal with physics and metaphysics alike.

February 21, 2018
BRUNO BÉRARD

PART I

Physics and Vertical Causation

The End of Quantum Reality

Wolfgang Smith

Preface

The present book is meant, in the first place, to serve as an introduction to a hitherto unrecognized mode of causation which proves moreover to be ubiquitous: what I refer to, namely, as "vertical causality." The question that immediately presents itself, of course, is how this newly-discovered causality relates to the causality with which physics has been concerned since the days of Sir Isaac Newton, which I shall refer to as "horizontal"; and suffice it to say, by way of a first orientation, that vertical causality does enter into the purview of physics, but in a manner the physicist as such is in principle unable to comprehend. For as we shall come to see, vertical causality—unlike horizontal—is not something quantitative, not something amenable to description in terms of differential equations. At the risk of producing more consternation than enlightenment, one could say that it is a causality that measures but cannot itself be measured. The crucial point is that even though the existence of vertical causation constitutes one of the two keys that render contemporary physics ontologically comprehensible, VC is something by nature invisible to the physicist, and hence proves to be *incurably* philosophical. It pertains moreover to a genre of philosophy which, in the post-Kantian era, has been quite out of fashion: to *metaphysics*. It is thus in a way ironic that this supposedly "outdated" discipline should emerge at the end of the twentieth century as the long sought-after means to understand the latest formulation of physics: that this philosophy should thus live up to its name as constituting indeed a *meta-physics*.

My second objective is to bring into unity the multiple strands pursued in the books I have written over the years, in a way that manifests what may rightfully be termed "the big picture." I take the liberty, moreover, to express myself sometimes in broad sweeps, leaving it to the interested reader to consult this or that earlier work, where a more detailed and documented account of a particular subject is to be found. One has, in the evening of one's life, the luxury to speak freely, and focus on what constitutes the most ultimately profound fact of all. At that point "lesser" facts hardly matter anymore in themselves. What counts in the end is an overview—like the panorama seen from a mountaintop—in which everything finds its rightful place, and "the many" mysteriously unite in that which is incomparably greater than their sum.

∾

Vertical causality made its appearance in the context of quantum theory, along with the ontological distinction between the physical and the corporeal domains. Not, to be sure, that it was "detected" in the sense of detecting a quantum particle! It is rather implied by virtue of the fact that the resolution of the so-called measurement problem demands as much.

What, then, *is* vertical causality? It needs to be recalled that the causality previously known to physics—which we now qualify as "horizontal"—acts *in time* by way of a temporal process; and as might thus be expected, *vertical* causality is characterized by the fact that it does *not* act in time: one can say that it acts *instantaneously.* How then can one ever "detect" an act of vertical causation: how, in other words, is it possible to conclude that an act of causation was actually *instantaneous* and not just "very fast"? That is where the distinction between ontological domains comes into play: if there exists indeed a *corporeal* domain—the one in which we "live, and move, and have our being"—as distinguished from the *physical* accessed by way of measurement, then it follows that the act of measurement entails a transition from the one to the other: and it is not difficult to see that an *ontological* transition can only be achieved instantaneously.

But whereas vertical causality was discovered in the context of quantum measurement, it proves to be ubiquitous: nothing whatsoever can in fact exist without being "vertically" caused. In particular, it is vertical causality that accounts for the ontological stratification of the cosmos—which the ancients understood so profoundly and present-day civilization fails even to recognize. There is the fact, first of all, that the corporeal world divides into the *mineral, plant, animal* and *anthropic* domains, which prove to be, once again, distinguished *ontologically*, and thus in ways physics as such cannot comprehend—for the very simple reason that, here again, what stands at issue are effects of vertical causality.

To comprehend this hitherto unrecognized mode of causation, we need to understand that the cosmos at large proves to be *ontologically trichotomous*: that even as man himself is made up of *corpus, anima,* and *spiritus,* so is the integral cosmos. Thus, as every major premodern civilization had recognized, there exist two additional ontological strata "above" the corporeal, rendering the cosmos tripartite.[1] There exists moreover a primordial iconic representation of that integral cosmos that proves to be invaluable, consisting quite simply of a circle in which the circumference corresponds to the corporeal world, the center to the spiritual or "celestial" realm, and the interior to the intermediary. What needs above all to be understood—and may indeed be termed the "hidden key"—is that *even as the corporeal domain is subject to the bounds of space and time, the intermediary is subject to time alone while the center is subject to neither of the two bounds.*[2] And so that center—that seeming "point," having neither extension in space nor duration in time, which thus appears to be "the least"—proves to be actually "the greatest of all"[3]: impervious to the constraints of space and the terminations of time, it encompasses in truth every "where" and every "when," and can therefore be identified as the *nunc stans,* the omnipresent "now that stands." Strange as it may seem so long as we picture it as something "far away and high above," that Apex is actually present within

---

1. Sanskrit may be the only language with a word for this ontological trichotomy, which is traditionally referred to in India as the *tribhuvāna* or "triple world."

2. I am not aware of any source which enunciates this fundamental principle. As a matter of fact, written sources, both ancient or modern, have precious little to say on the subject of such a "cosmic icon." What we do find are *clues.* A study on this subject would be of great interest.

3. I would note parenthetically that the correspondence here with various allusions in the New Testament—for instance, the parable of the mustard seed—is by no means accidental or adventitious.

every being as its ultimate center. This means that every actual being is endowed with an ontological "within" centered upon that Apex: it is as if the two centers actually "touch."[4]

To the Thomist let me point out that for every cosmic being, that "meeting point" may be identified with its substantial form. It is needful, therefore, to distinguish between the two centers: the one universal Center (represented by the central point of the cosmic icon), and the other definitive of a cosmic existent. What concerns us is the fact that vertical causality, by virtue of not acting "in time," acts necessarily from a center, and therefore in one of two ways: it may act from the universal Center, in which case that causality coincides with the cosmogenetic Act, or from the center of a particular being, in which case—so far from being cosmogenetic—it is evidently the act of a cosmic agent. And needless to say, there exists a very broad spectrum of such cosmic activity, ranging from the existential act of a pebble to the free and creative acts of man.

Let me, at this juncture, assure the reader that "the worst" is now over: having plunged ahead into admittedly abstruse and difficult realms—to provide a kind of synoptic overview of the territory we are about to enter—we shall henceforth proceed by clear and simple steps. My aim in this monograph is to provide a readily comprehensible—and exceedingly brief—introduction to the discovery and the implications of vertical causality, extending our purview step by step from quantum physics to the cosmos at large: for as we have seen, vertical causality acts in truth from that "*punto dello stelo a cui la prima rota va ditorno*"—from that "*pivot around which the primordial wheel revolves*," to put it in Dante's inimitable words. "*There*

---

4. As the reader may note, in the special case of the *anthropos* that "within" coincides with what mystics are wont to call the "heart." It should likewise be noted that the cosmic icon applies not only to the cosmos at large—traditionally termed the *macrocosm*—but likewise to man, the so-called *microcosm*, an analogy which in fact it exemplifies.

every where and every when are focused,"[5] the Poet goes on to say by way of depicting that central and yet ubiquitous *punto dello stelo* wherein the mystery of vertical causation resides.

❧

It remains to say that I am highly honored to co-author a book with Professor Jean Borella, one of the greatest authorities in the field of authentic metaphysics, ranging from the ancient schools of East and West through the great Christian era down to its contemporary decline, the symptoms and causes of which he understands perhaps more profoundly than anyone else. As the reader will clearly discern, Professor Borella's contribution and mine—though both deal, as they should, with *"physique et métaphysique"*—prove to be profoundly different. For whereas Professor Borella's essay takes its starting point in metaphysics to engage with physics, mine commences at the level of physics to engage with metaphysics. It seems to me, moreover, that these respective inquiries do not simply constitute two different ways of approaching a common question, but answer to different needs: in the case of Jean Borella, it is the need on the part of the metaphysician to comprehend science metaphysically, whereas in mine it is the need of the scientist to open his eyes to higher and incomparably more profound realms: the immeasurable vistas, namely, upon which sages meditate.

---

5. *Paradiso* xiii, 10 and xxix, 12.

1

The Origin
of Quantum Theory

T he story begins in the fateful year 1900 when a young physicist named Max Planck decided to investigate the so-called black-body problem. It has always been known that a piece of iron, for example, glows red; yet for some unknown reason it turned out that calculations invariably indicated that it ought to glow blue. Now, to calculate the radiation of a black-body, one needs to relate the kinetic energy E of a vibrating particle to the light-frequency f it emits; and what Planck discovered—serendipitously as it turns out—is that this emission can take place only in "packets" of energy given by hf, where h is a constant subsequently referred to as "the quantum of action" or Planck's constant. Its value has since been established to be 6.626076 times 10 to the power −34 (in standard units); and thus emended, the theory yields the values confirmed by experiment.

As might be expected, this result proved to be utterly incomprehensible to the physics community at the time, and it is safe to say that no one as yet had the ghost of an idea what Planck's discovery presaged. The conviction was rife that physics had attained a state of near-perfection in which only minor problems remained yet to be resolved—which is why the young Planck had in fact been advised by his mentors not to become a physicist, but to pursue instead a career in music! It happens, however, that this state of affairs was about to change.

Since the days of Sir Isaac Newton it had been supposed that matter reduces ultimately to Democritean atoms, and that with the refinement of experimental means these would eventually present themselves as objects to be measured and observed. However, at the very moment when this prospect did materialize, it became apparent that these so-called atoms are not in fact "tiny particles" at all. In place of authentic atoms, what came to light is something that exhibits both particle and wave characteristics, which is to say that it is actually neither a particle nor a wave. Thus, if we do think of it as a particle, we must live with the fact that it can, for example, pass through two slits in a partition at the same time, and can moreover "multilocate" in countless other ways. Nor do we fare any better if we conceive of these entities as "waves," inasmuch as it is now the particle-aspect that does not fit.

One was left thus with something that can no longer be pictured or conceived at all—except possibly in mathematical terms. By the time the "smoke had cleared," physicists were obliged to accept the fact that their near-perfect Newtonian science had, in a sense, vanished into thin air. Of course the theory could still be applied to technology in domains where the deviation from classical behavior is insignificant (which of course covers a very broad range); but that, in any case, is all that remains of the two-century-long Newtonian hegemony.

It was a singularly exciting and challenging time. What was needed was not only a brand new physics that works, but also a new understanding of what physics *is*: that is to say, how it relates to reality. And as we shall come to see, the first of these objectives the physics community was able to achieve rapidly and to perfection, whereas the second they have not been able to attain at all. It thus came about that the most perfect physics the world had ever seen turned out to be "a kind of mystic chant over an unintelligible universe," in Whitehead's telling words.

Let us take a summary look at this new physics. As we have seen, the entities—if indeed that term is still applicable—with which it is concerned exhibit both wave and particle aspects, which implies that in truth they answer to neither designation. It turns out, moreover, that a strict determinism is no longer tenable: somehow the notion of "probability" *must* enter the picture—for it is precisely an "indeterminacy" that allows wave and particle characteristics to co-exist without logical contradiction. The fact is that quantum physics needs both the wave and the particle representation, together with a "principle of indeterminacy" to render them compatible. On top of which it needs one more ingredient: a means, namely, of passing from one to the other. And this is where Planck's constant comes into play: in connecting the *energy* of a vibrating particle to the *frequency* of a wave, it serves as the bridge between the two descriptions.

What was called for, as we have said, was a brand new physics; and amazingly, that transition was accomplished—to perfection!— in a span of twenty-five years. A veritable explosion of genius ensued, such as the world had rarely seen; and in the fateful year 1925—in one giant leap as it were—physics attained what might well be its ultimate form. The discovery was in fact made three times, in terms of three radically dissimilar mathematical structures which later proved to be isomorphic. It was by any count a stellar moment in the history of man's quest to comprehend the universe.

In a way, the greatest genius among the three discoverers was Werner Heisenberg, a 24-year-old physicist and close friend of Niels Bohr, who in July of 1925 sojourned on the desolate isle of Helgoland. Finding himself alone—the sea before him and the sky above—the young physicist was apparently seized by a spirit of "back to the facts." It struck him thus that whereas physicists at large invariably evinced boundless respect for the so-called "hard facts of observation," they seemed rarely to ask themselves what these facts might actually be. They seemed to assume, in particular, that a physical system owns its dynamic attributes—a position or momentum, say—prior to the act of measurement, when in fact this constitutes evidently an unverifiable hypothesis. One may presume that Heisenberg was moved to ask himself whether this may not prove to be indeed the very assumption that renders us incapable of understanding the quantum world! And perhaps, at this juncture, he recalled Lord Kelvin's definition of physics as "the science of measurement"—and realized in a flash that *the mystery of quantum physics resides precisely in the act of measurement itself.*

What we do know is that, abandoning the aforesaid assumption, Heisenberg—in the course of a single day and night—invented a mathematical formalism[1] that enables one to transact the business of physics without assuming that quantum systems own their dynamic attributes. Briefly stated, what a quantum system owns in place of actual dynamic attributes, according to Heisenberg's theory, is an array of probabilities, which could be represented as the elements of an infinite matrix. And unwieldy as the resultant "matrix mechanics" may be, it has now been in direct or indirect use for close to a century and has never yet yielded a false result. It would not be unreasonable to suggest that, here at last, physics has attained its ultimate ground in the form of a mathematical science which fully squares with the corresponding facts.

The idea obtrudes that Heisenberg's quantum theory could be something "given" or "discovered" rather than "man-made"; and it appears that Heisenberg himself may have shared that view. As his wife Elisabeth recalls: "With smiling certainty, he once said to me 'I was lucky enough to be allowed once to look over the good Lord's shoulder while he was at work.' That was enough for him, more than enough!"[2]

---

1. Strictly speaking, he "re-invented" that formalism: what stands at issue is the algebraic theory of matrices, with which the young Heisenberg was not acquainted at the time.

2. Elisabeth Heisenberg, *Inner Exile: Recollections of a Life with Werner Heisenberg* (Boston: Birkhäuser, 1980), 157.

2

The Quantum Enigma

Yet it appears that the consummate perfection of quantum theory comes at a price: for it happens that no one seems to have so much as the slightest notion what in plain fact it means—whether, for example, there actually exists a "quantum world" or not. Now it seems that physicists at large have not been unduly disturbed by this state of affairs. Most seem content to vacillate between the pre-quantum outlook on the one hand and some suitably reified picture of the quantum realm. They appear for the most part not even to realize that something is seriously amiss, and that in fact they are pendulating between two contradictory worldviews. In the upper echelons of the physics community, on the other hand, efforts began almost immediately to render the marvelous new physics intelligible as well. For that subclass of physicists who are more than technicians, predicting the outcome of experiments was not enough; they wanted also to understand what physics entails regarding the actual composition of the world, and found it intolerable that the new science seemed not to fit the prevailing worldview. A debate concerning these deeper issues began almost immediately at the Solvay Conference of 1927 in the form of the famous Bohr-Einstein exchange, and for the past ninety years, to be precise, physicists with a philosophic bent have proposed and counter-proposed the most extraordinary notions in an effort to resolve the persisting riddle, *with no resolution yet in sight.* It appears that Richard Feynman may well have hit the nail on the head with his apodictic declaration *"No one understands quantum theory."* Many do, of course, understand the theory on a technical plane: the *"no one"* applies—not evidently when one compares mathematical solutions with corresponding measurements—but the moment one asks how a red apple in our hand relates to protons and electrons.

As concerns the manifold proposals put forth by physicists in the interminable quest to resolve the "quantum reality" conundrum, it needs first of all to be noted that, in the final count, each without exception falls short of the mark. On the whole these proposals strike the "unprogrammed" observer as ranging—let me speak plainly—from the bizarre to the outright ridiculous, and none more so, I would add, than the so-called "many-worlds" approach which seeks to rescue determinism by stipulating that every possible outcome of every measurement is in fact realized, *howbeit in a different universe!* So too mention might be made of the so-called "quantum logic" approach, based upon the remarkable premise that ordinary logic ceases to apply in the quantum realm. The very absurdity of such proposals—combined with the fact that they originated in universities and institutes for advanced study—serves to underscore the difficulty and indeed profundity of the quantum enigma.

I shall argue that it is the so-called Copenhagen interpretation, originally conceived by Niels Bohr, that *beyond all doubt* holds precedence over all competing views regarding the nature of quantum reality by virtue of its pivotal tenet, which affirms that *a quantum system does not own its dynamic attributes* (such as position or momentum). As previously noted, this was in essence the "back to the facts" recognition which inspired Heisenberg, on that fateful day in 1925, to achieve his monumental breakthrough. Meanwhile that stipulation was confirmed, in 1932, by a Hungarian mathematician named John von Neumann, in a startling revelation which appeared to settle the issue beyond all doubt. What von Neumann accomplished breaks into two parts: first, he axiomatized the principles of quantum physics, thereby putting the discipline upon a rigorous mathematical foundation, following which he showed that the Copenhagenist claim of no "pre-measured" dynamic attributes can now be established as a mathematical theorem. Thus, if we define an *ordinary* object as one that owns its dynamic attributes, the theorem states quite simply that *there are no* ordinary objects in the quantum realm.

But whereas it appeared at this point that the matter had now been settled once and for all, it turns out that additional feats of genius were in the offing, which would, once again, upset the *status quo.* For it turns out that von Neumann had neglected to spell out a certain condition that had hitherto been assumed as a matter of course, but which proves ultimately to be not only unwarranted but indeed untenable. Which brings us to John Stuart Bell, the physicist who, in 1964, in the course of an exacting study of von Neumann's proof, identified that mysterious condition. What von Neumann had tacitly assumed—and what later came to be known as the condition of *locality*—is that quantum particles can interact only via forces which propagate no faster than the speed of light. It thus turns out that what von Neumann had actually established as a theorem of quantum mechanics is that *local* objects do not own their dynamic attributes: which is to say that *ordinary objects must be nonlocal.*

From the outset the epicenter of the quantum reality debate was defined by the Bohr-Einstein exchange. Quantum theory had scarcely seen the light of day when the renowned Albert Einstein stepped forth to challenge Niels Bohr in a bid to overthrow the new physics, or at the very least, reduce it to a mere approximation "beneath" which a basically Einsteinian physics reigns supreme. What troubled Einstein the most in regard to quantum theory, it seems, is the loss of a Newtonian or "absolute" determinism, that is to say, its replacement by an incurably *probabilistic* physics; as he famously put it: "*God does not play dice.*" Moreover, inasmuch as an absolute determinism demands "ordinary" objects, Einstein was adamantly opposed to the central tenet of the Copenhagenist position. He consequently proposed various arguments and a plethora of ingenious experiments designed to reinstate ordinary objects in a bid to disprove the quantum-mechanical indeterminism. The irony is that one of these—the so-called Einstein-Podolski-Rosen or EPR experiment—has led eventually to a result henceforth known as Bell's theorem, which constitutes arguably an irrefutable *disproof* of Einstein's contention.

To indicate briefly what stands at issue, let us consider a somewhat simplified version of the relevant EPR experiment. Consider two photons in a so-called "state of parallel polarization," emanating in opposite directions from a source O to points A and B, which can be as widely separated as we wish. Whereas neither particle possesses a definite polarization initially, this entails that once a polarization has been established by an act of measurement at A (let us say), the same polarization will be found in the photon at B: it is as if the measurement at A effects the state of the photon at B *instantaneously*. Thus, if one can still speak of "interaction" at all, what confronts us here is indeed a *nonlocal* interaction: the kind von Neumann had inadvertently left out of account. And so his famous theorem, as we have noted before, does not in fact rule out *ordinary* objects *per se*—as everyone had initially believed—but only *local* ordinary objects: the kind that interact only via forces carried by fields.

This brings us finally to what has come to be known as Bell's theorem, an epochal result the Irish physicist discovered in the wake of his inquiry into von Neumann's proof. By means of an argument inspired by the EPR setup, and which, though ingenious in the extreme, turns out to be relatively uncomplicated, Bell proved—to everyone's utter amazement!—that actually *there are no local objects:* in a word: *reality is nonlocal.* Now the implications of this discovery prove to be unimaginably far-reaching, and for the most part remain yet to be explored. Meanwhile, one would be hard pressed not to concur with Berkeley physicist Henry Stapp when he declares Bell's theorem to be "the most profound discovery of science."[1]

The question now becomes what Bell's theorem has to say regarding Einstein's view of quantum theory. It is true that *ordinary* objects have not in fact been ruled out, as von Neumann's theorem had initially seemed to imply. But meanwhile something no less unacceptable to Einsteinians has come to light: the fact, namely, that *physical objects*—including the *ordinary* kind, if such do in fact

---

1. "Bell's Theorem and World Process," *Il Nuovo Cimento*, 40b (1977), 271. For a readable explanation of Bell's proof we refer to Nick Herbert, *Quantum Reality* (New York: Doubleday, 1985), 211–31.

exist—*must be nonlocal*: have the capacity, that is, to communicate with other such objects *instantaneously*, a possibility which the very axioms of relativistic physics stringently exclude. The irony is that it was the EPR set-up—which Einstein himself had conceived in the expectation that it would disprove the claims of quantum theory—that had enabled Bell to prove his "anti-Einsteinian" theorem.

∾

Getting back to the interpretation of quantum theory: the superiority of the Copenhagen approach, I would argue, derives from its care not to overstep the bounds of what we actually know: only in the wake of such an over-reach, I surmise, does one experience a need for something as weird as a "multiverse" or a so-called "quantum logic." As Niels Bohr reminds us, even to speak of a "quantum world" is to overstep what we actually know: a "quantum description" is all we can legitimately claim. And that description is moreover geared to the business of physics: beyond this, its intended and rightful application, no one indeed "understands quantum theory"! It was the philosopher Alfred North Whitehead—and not Niels Bohr—who lamented the fact that physics has thus been reduced to "a mystic chant over an unintelligible universe." How quantum physics could be more than a "mystic chant"—that problem remained yet to be resolved.

3

Finding the Hidden Key

Not long after I had begun to peruse the quantum reality literature, I was struck by the fact that everyone seemed implicitly to presuppose a major philosophic postulate, which at the very least could be characterized as "dubious." Whereas, as a rule, assumptions of even the most seemingly innocuous kind were sought out meticulously and subjected to exacting scrutiny by one or another of the quantum-reality theorists—even the hitherto sacrosanct principles of logic!—I was amazed to find that the Cartesian premises, which entered the scientific mainstream by way of Newton's *Principia*, had apparently remained undetected, and in any case unchallenged by the investigators. What stands at issue in this philosophic Ansatz is a splitting of the real into two mutually exclusive compartments: an external world comprised of so-called *res extensae* or "extended entities," and an internal and subjective domain consisting of *res cogitantes* or "thinking entities." And even though this Cartesian "bifurcation" has been often enough called into question by philosophers of rank, and Alfred North Whitehead in particular has chided the scientific community repeatedly for its adhesion to what he termed "the fallacy of misplaced concreteness," it appears these strictures have invariably fallen upon deaf ears. Whitehead himself, moreover, offers at least one explanation as to why the Cartesian philosophy has thus become *de facto* sacrosanct:

> In the first place, we must note its astounding efficiency as a system of concepts for the organization of scientific research.... Every university in the world organizes itself in accordance with it.

No alternative system of organizing the pursuit of scientific truth has been suggested. It is not only reigning, but it is without a rival. And yet—it is quite unbelievable.[1]

One might add that these words were written prior to 1925, the year when everything pertaining to physics changed—or should by right have changed. When it comes to "the system without rival" however, what came to pass was a classic case of "pouring new wine into old bottles": Cartesian bottles, to be exact.

The main exception among the reigning authorities, it seems, was Werner Heisenberg, who did at times voice doubts concerning the Cartesian postulates, and lamented that "today in the physics of elementary particles, good physics is unconsciously being spoiled by bad philosophy."[2] Now, it seemed to me that what was actually being "spoiled" by that "bad philosophy" was not in fact the "good physics" itself, but the *ontological interpretation* of that "good physics," which is something else entirely. And so I arrived at the surmise that it must be, at bottom, the Cartesian partition of the real into *res extensae* and *res cogitantes* that accounts for the fact that, to this day, "*no one understands quantum theory.*"

The first thing that needed to be done to break the Cartesian stranglehold was to see how the postulate of bifurcation stands on philosophic ground: whether, in other words, it is well founded. What struck me was the fact that, in essence, Descartes had simply reinstated the Democritean atomism—the notion that "*there exist color, the sweet and the bitter, but in reality only atoms and the void*"[3] as the celebrated fragment has it—a doctrine which the major schools of Greek philosophy came in time to view as heterodox. The key issue, it seemed to me, is to grasp how sense perception—and *visual* perception above all—can transcend the subjective realm of *res cogitantes* so as to perceive, not a mere image, but indeed the external object itself: the world of *res extensae*. And so, in the first chapter of *The Quantum Enigma*, I dealt with this question as best I

1. *Science and the Modern World* (New York: Macmillan, 1925), 54.

2. *Encounters with Einstein* (Princeton University Press, 1983), 81.

3. Hermann Diels, *Fragmente der Vorsokratiker* (Dublin: Wiedemann, 1969), vol. II, 168.

could—unaware of the fact that, not long before, a cognitive psychologist by the name of James Gibson had in effect resolved this issue on rigorous scientific ground. To be precise: having discovered, by means of key experiments, that the prevailing "visual image" theory of perception proves to be untenable, and having subsequently spent three decades in quest of a new paradigm, Gibson arrived at what he terms "the ecological theory of visual perception," which—incredible as it may seem—*falsifies* the Cartesian premise *on scientific grounds*, and re-establishes what amounts to the pre-Cartesian realism.[4] We will recur to this crucial issue in the next chapter.

Given then that we do perceive the external world—that the grass is actually green and the red apple in my hand is not after all a *res cogitans*—given this fundamental premise, I posed the question whether it is possible to interpret physics *per se*, based on its inherent *modus operandi*, in non-bifurcationist terms. And let it be noted at once: if such be indeed the case, it follows that *the non-bifurcationist interpretation of physics cannot be rejected on scientific grounds*. Or to put it another way: if indeed it is possible to transact the business of physics on a non-bifurcationist basis, then—contrary to the prevailing belief—Cartesian bifurcation is bereft of scientific support. *The contemporary Weltanschauung—which implicitly assumes bifurcation to be a scientific fact—has then been disproved.*

Such was the plan; and its execution proved to be surprisingly uncomplicated. The first and crucial step was to distinguish *ontologically* between *corporeal* and *physical* objects, based upon the fact that these answer to fundamentally different ways of knowing: to direct perception on the one hand, and to the *modus operandi* of physics on the other. *Corporeal* objects, then, are the kind we perceive, whereas things *physical* are the kind we know by empirical means, i.e., by way of *mensuration*. And these categories define two distinct ontological planes: the *corporeal*, which is accessed by way of sense perception, and the *physical*, which has come into view

---

4. James Gibson, *The Ecological Theory of Visual Perception* (Hillsdale, NJ: Erlbaum Publications, 1986). I have discussed Gibson's theory at length in *Science and Myth* (Tacoma, WA: Angelico Press/Sophia Perennis, 2012), ch. 4.

through the discoveries of physics.[5] I would add that I regard the ontological distinction between these two planes to be crucial for the resolution of the quantum enigma: that in fact a philosophic comprehension of the quantum realm hinges precisely upon that recognition.

But let us continue: inasmuch as we find ourselves thus confronted by two distinct ontological planes, the economy of physics demands the existence of a bridge which enables us to pass from one to the other, in the absence of which there evidently could be no physical science at all. Now it turns out that there exists one and only one such bridge, which unbeknownst to the scientific community has been in constant use since the days of Newton: what then is that "invisible" connecting link? It is defined by the function S which to every corporeal object X assigns the corresponding *physical* object SX, which is simply *X as conceived by the physicist*. But let us not fail to note that X and SX prove to be as different as night and day: the corporeal object X has color, for example, and owns a host of other *qualitative* attributes (failing which it could not be perceived), not one of which pertains to SX by virtue of the fact that the latter is described exclusively in mathematical terms. It is moreover to be noted that the "bridge" is crossed from X to SX by the theoretician, and again from SX to X by the experimentalist in the act of measurement. *The economy of physics hinges thus upon two "crossings" of that bridge:* a theoretical transition from X to SX, complemented by an empirical return from SX to X.

These, then, are the basic conceptions that enable a non-bifurcationist interpretation of physics; and let me emphasize that what is thus specified is not a particular *kind* of physics, but physics *per se* as defined by its founding *modus operandi*. That interpretation is consequently immune from contradiction on scientific grounds: it sim-

---

5. There is reason to believe that, to some extent at least, the physical universe is actually "constructed" by the intervention of the physicist, which is the reason John Wheeler refers to it as "the participatory universe," and why Heisenberg states that physics deals, not with Nature as such, but with "our relations to Nature." I have dealt with this issue at length in "Eddington and the Primacy of the Corporeal." See *Ancient Wisdom and Modern Misconceptions* (Kettering, OH: Angelico Press/Sophia Perennis, 2015), ch. 2.

ply brings to light what exactly physics *is*, and what *kind* of knowledge it supplies. The primary reference of physics, it thus turns out, is not in fact to the corporeal world, but to the physical domain, which proves moreover to be actualized by its own *modus operandi*. The reason why physics does nonetheless have something to say regarding the *corporeal* realm resides in the fact that the latter derives its *quantitative* content from the *physical*. One may, of course, go on to ask all manner of questions concerning the nature and origin of that "subcorporeal" domain, its relation to other ontological strata, and so forth: the point, however, is that these are *philosophic* questions which physics as such is neither able nor in any way obliged to answer.

∾

We need now to ask what it is that distinguishes the corporeal from the physical; and the first thing to note is that this, too, is a question physical science as such cannot pose, let alone answer. *Physics has eyes only for the physical*, period; and one might add that inestimable harm to civilization at large has resulted from the fact that this inherently obvious fact has as a rule been negated by the presiding elite. The almost universal tendency on the part of physicists to conflate the physical and the corporeal domains turns out thus to constitute a category error resulting from a failure to comprehend the *modus operandi* of physics in ontological terms.

What in truth distinguishes corporeal entities from the physical is the fact that they exist. This may of course come as a shock to the public at large inasmuch as the prevailing worldview affirms in effect the very opposite. In the name of science an uncanny deception has been imposed upon humanity, which—quite literally—*stands the world on its head.* Yet the fact remains that *the physical,* properly so called—so far from coinciding with the corporeal—constitutes in truth a *sub-existential* domain. And this should in fact come as no surprise if only one recalls that Heisenberg himself has situated the so-called elementary particles ontologically "just in the middle between possibility and reality," and has pointed out that as such they are in fact "reminiscent of Aristotelian *potentiae*."[6] We need thus to ask the crucial question: what is it, then, that *actualizes* these *potentiae*? And as is so often the case when, at long last, the right question is posed: the answer stares us in the face! *Quantum particles are "actualized" precisely in the act of measurement*, and thus *on the corporeal plane*: in the state of a *corporeal* instrument, to be exact.

The key to the quantum enigma is thus to be found in Lord Kelvin's conception of physics as "*the science of measurement*," which is to say that the ultimate object of physics is neither the physical as such, much less the corporeal, but the transition, precisely, from the former to the latter in the act of measurement. A so-called quantum particle, thus, is not *actually* a particle—does not, properly speaking, *exist!*—until it interacts with a corporeal instrument of measurement or detection: "beneath" the corporeal plane all is potency, what Heisenberg refers to as "Aristotelian *potentiae*." In the final count, one is forced to admit that the *physical* universe, properly so called, constitutes, properly speaking, a *sub-existential* domain, which in an unimaginably subtle yet absolutely precise sense *underlies* the corporeal world, and in fact determines its *quantitative* attributes.

We should remind ourselves, at this juncture, that the notion of an ontological realm or stratum "*beneath*" the corporeal proves to be integral to our metaphysical heritage. It springs in fact from the seminal recognition that corporeal being entails, not one, but *two* fundamental principles: something called *hyle* or *materia*, plus *morphe* or *form*, to put it in Aristotelian terms. Everything in creation hinges upon these two complementary principles: the *paternal*, exemplified by *form*, and the *maternal* corresponding to *materia* (it seems our very language testifies to this fact). The doctrine known

6. *Physics and Philosophy* (New York: Harper & Row, 1962), 41.

as *hylomorphism* proves thus to be—not the mere invention of Aristotle—but the expression of a universal truth, which in one form or another constitutes in fact the *sine qua non* of every sound ontology.

It will be expedient at this point to observe that this foundational duality of *form* and *matter* has been conceived *iconically*—from time immemorial—as a *vertical* distinction, which is to say that one conceives of *morphe* "pictorially" as situated "above" *materia*, a step which defines a "vertical" axis, a cosmic "up" and "down," a "high" and "low." It is hard to describe or explain what actually stands at issue here because the idea is incurably metaphysical, and yet so very "cosmic," so very "pictorial" one could even say. Yet the fact is that the authentic concept of "verticality" is both factual and normative, a universal compass one might say, accessible to mankind. I therefore ask the reader's indulgence: bear with me when I speak of "verticality"—of "high" and "low"—in so many contexts, while insisting that these are not merely "subjective" conceptions. More than that is in play: what stands at issue, in the final count, *is nothing less than the metaphysical foundation of the world*, which resides in the *morphe/hyle* dichotomy.[7]

In terms of this metaphysical and archetypal symbolism we can "picture" the integral cosmos as a hierarchy of "horizontal" planes;[8] which brings us to the question: where then—on what "level"—are we to situate this, our *corporeal* world? And contrary to contemporary expectation, metaphysical tradition answers with one voice: *on the very lowest tier!* According to the simplest and if you will primary representation, we arrive thus at three tiers—corresponding, as we have noted before, to the *corpus-anima-spiritus* ternary. The corporeal plane of the integral cosmos corresponds thus to the "corporeal" component of man. This is where "existence," properly so

---

7. I cannot refrain from pointing out that it is precisely the loss of this metaphysical recognition that has led to the well-nigh universal relativism in regard to values and norms of every "non-quantitative" kind, be it in the sphere of art, morality, or, of course, religion. The idea that "values" are ultimately founded upon *truth* is perhaps the contra-modern recognition most desperately needed in our day.

8. Or as concentric rings, in accordance with what we have termed, in the preface, the "cosmic icon."

called, comes to an end—or begins, if you look at it the other way. *Below* the corporeal world there is "pure *materia*," so-called *materia prima*, conceived as a "pure receptivity" which as such does not actually exist.

Now, all this having been said, we can return to the quantum enigma and state, quite simply, that the physical universe is situated *below* the corporeal, or more precisely: "between" the corporeal and *materia prima*. One might add that this prime or first *"materia"* corresponds to the so-called "waters" over which *"the spirit of God"* was said to "move"—or even more suggestively, perhaps, to the *Chaos* which, according to Hesiod, *"was in the beginning."* These in any case are the metaphysical categories, come down to us from remote antiquity, in terms of which one can "situate" the newly-discovered quantum world. To do so in terms of concepts less ancient and less venerable would prove, I believe, to be misconceived.

I would add—for those who have "eyes to see"—that these ancient and perhaps pre-historic cosmological conceptions carry not only an archetypal, but a *mystical* sense impenetrable to the modern mind. Yet even so we can draw inspiration from that perennial source, and *need in fact to do so* if ever we are to "understand quantum theory." It might be worth pointing out that Hesiod's allusion to a sub-existential *Chaos*—which can after all be conceived as a kind of co-presence of contradictory elements—may not be irrelevant to the metaphysics of quantum theory, which does after all entail a "co-presence" of mutually exclusive states[9] by virtue of the superposition principle. Could it be, then, that the quantum realm rests upon or embodies that Hesiodian *Chaos*? What in any case has been established beyond doubt through the resolution of the quantum enigma is that the quantum world—or more precisely, what I term the *physical universe*—proves to be a sub-existential domain, situated ontologically between *prima materia* and the corporeal plane.

---

9. As distinguished from an actual coexistence, which would be antinomous.

∾

Having thus "situated" the physical or quantum world, it is crucial to note that in this subcorporeal realm the concept of "substance" ceases to apply: as Arthur Eddington was quick to recognize: "*the concept of substance*" has indeed "*disappeared from fundamental physics.*"[10] The problem, however, is that so far hardly anyone, even within the academic ranks, appears to have grasped the point: to this day the tendency to reify the quantum world *at the expense of the corporeal*—as a mark of up-to-date enlightenment, no less!—is rife across the land. I recall with consternation, but little surprise, the words of a top Vatican spokesman, who announced that the concept of "transubstantiation" is no longer tenable "because physics has proved that there is no such thing as *substance*." It is time, I say, to put an end to this catastrophic confusion, imposed upon present-day humanity by the reigning *periti*: high time, indeed, to recover our collective sanity!

To this end let it be recalled, once again, that this intellectual—and spiritual—bedlam is based squarely upon Cartesian bifurcation, which to this day serves as the bedrock of our supposedly "scientific" Weltanschauung. It is astounding to observe what a veritable stranglehold this unlikely and indeed untenable premise exerts to this day upon our post-Newtonian civilization: how the most basic tenets our science is said to have "proved" rest squarely upon that illusory foundation.

What is it then, of which Cartesian bifurcation has in effect deprived the external world, that mankind so desperately needs? What could it be, in the absence of which we lose our bearing and become progressively dehumanized? The answer to this vital question is that the precious ingredient is given to us in the apprehension of what we have termed *verticality*: in the fact, namely, that the cosmos presentifies not only entities, but *values*, that it speaks to us not only of "things," but of *beauty* and *goodness*—and ultimately, as Plato informs us, of the Beautiful and the Good itself. We need to

<hr>

10. *The Philosophy of Physical Science* (Cambridge University Press, 1949), 110.

remind ourselves thus of the categorical distinction between *qualities* and *quantities*, which proves to be immeasurably profound: for whereas *quantities* derive in truth "from below"—in keeping with the Scholastic dictum *"numerus stat ex parte materiae"*—it can in truth be said that *qualities* stem "from above," that in fact *they transmit the light of supernal essences into this nether world.*

It thus becomes evident—on the basis of what might truly be termed *the perennial wisdom of mankind*—that in banishing the *qualitative* content of the corporeal world by relegating qualities *per se* to a subjective realm of so-called *res cogitantes*, Descartes has in effect cast out the very *essence* of the world in which we live, and move, and have our being. The crucial and almost universally undiscerned fact is that the Cartesian reduction of the corporeal world to "matter"—the denial, thus, of its "formal" component, its inherent *morphe*—has seemingly emptied the world of everything that answers to the higher cravings of the human heart. And of all that has thus been forfeited, *the loss of the sacred* is beyond doubt the most tragic of all: for that proves to be the privation we cannot ultimately survive.

Meanwhile—in the wake of the Cartesian disclosure—it seemed to the dazzled progeny of the Enlightenment that every new triumph of Newtonian physics constituted yet another proof of that *non plus ultra* Weltanschauung. And so the victorious march continued right up to the twentieth century, at which point something utterly unexpected occurred: at the precise moment when that all-conquering physics finally attained to its own ground by ridding itself of its last non-quantitative vestiges, it came to pass that the very idea of "substance"—and thus of *being*—had to be jettisoned: in the so-called "quantum world" there *is* no substance, no *being* whatsoever! And from that point onwards, as we have seen, physicists have been confronted by the daunting task of constructing a universe out of "things" that do not actually exist: no wonder that labor continues up to the present day!

Given that Descartes propounded his fateful postulate to prepare the way for a mathematical physics of unlimited scope, it is ironic that the very science to which that Ansatz gave rise has led in the end to a veritable *reductio ad absurdum* which in effect disqualifies the Cartesian worldview itself. Thus it came to pass in 1897—just when the quest for *res extensae* in the form of Democritean atoms seemed finally to have attained its end in J. J. Thomson's discovery of the electron—that at this very moment the long-sought quarry mysteriously eluded our grasp. And by 1925, following one of the most intense periods of intellectual endeavor in human history, the verdict was in: *there is actually no such thing as a "fundamental particle,"* no such thing as a *res extensa* at all! One might add that the nonexistence of *res extensae* could indeed have been foreseen by anyone conversant with the traditions of metaphysics; what proves to have been humanly unforeseeable, on the other hand, is the discovery of a subcorporeal domain, made up of entities "midway between being and nonbeing," from whence the *quantitative* attributes of the corporeal universe are derived, along with a mathematical physics of unimaginable accuracy descriptive of this realm, which gives rise moreover to technological wonders that not only *"could deceive even the elect,"*[11] but arguably have done so.

Getting back to the quantum enigma: it needs now to be pointed out that what I have termed "the rediscovery of the corporeal world" proves to be but the first step in the resolution of the quantum quandary. What is likewise required, it turns out—in addition to a supra-physical world—is a supra-physical mode of causation. Thus, in addition to the modes of causality with which physical science is conversant—which operate by way of a temporal process that may be deterministic, random or stochastic, and which we shall henceforth refer to as *"horizontal"*—there exists also what I term a

---

11. Matt. 24:24.

vertical mode of causality, which does *not* operate in time, but acts *instantaneously* and therefore, as it were, "above time." It turns out, moreover, that this hitherto unrecognized causality plays a crucial role in the economy of physics, and thus constitutes yet another reason why "nobody understands quantum theory."

As the ontological distinction between the *physical* and the *corporeal* might lead one to surmise, it is precisely in the act of measurement that *vertical* causation comes perforce into play. For it stands to reason that *horizontal causation cannot act from one ontological plane to another*—given that such an effect must be *instantaneous*. Inasmuch, therefore, as the act of measurement does entail an interaction between the *physical* system and a *corporeal* instrument, it cannot be attributed to horizontal causation: the matter turns out to be as simple as that! The fact is that, at the instant of measurement, the evolution of the physical system, as described say by the Schrödinger wave equation, is interrupted—the Schrödinger equation is "re-initialized," as physicists say—an event for which there is no *physical* explanation. In fact, there *cannot* be: what confronts us here proves incontrovertibly to constitute an effect of *vertical* causation, an act which affects both the measuring instrument and the physical system *instantaneously*. It should be noted, moreover, that this causation "emanates," not from the physical, but perforce from the corporeal side, inasmuch as it interrupts—or "overrides"—the "Schrödinger causality" indigenous to the physical plane.

I would point out, moreover, that this settles the long-debated question whether the postulate of a perfect or so-called "Lagrangian" determinism has or has not been disqualified by quantum theory: it can in fact be seen that it has, though not on purely mathematical grounds. For insofar as the act of measurement entails an ontological transition from the physical to the corporeal domain, it cannot be fully described in mathematical terms: no differential equation, evidently, can determine the outcome of an *instantaneous* act! And let us note that this interdict refers in particular to the differential equations of de Broglie-Bohm theory, which despite their marvelous elegance and rigor of mathematical derivation still do not apply to an act that does not transpire in time. The ineluctable verdict, thus, is that the notion of a Lagrangian or "mathematical" determinism has now been rigorously disqualified, *and no "hidden variables" theory can alter this fact.*

Getting back to vertical causation: one recognition, as is so often the case, leads to another. Even as the rediscovery of the corporeal domain has led to the identification of vertical causality in the act of measurement, it now becomes apparent that other acts of VC are occurring ubiquitously, beginning with the fact that every corporeal object X acts "vertically" upon the corresponding physical object SX—which is evidently the reason why cricket balls don't multilocate and cats cannot be both dead and alive.[12] The point is that the physical object SX is invariably constrained by its corporeal counterpart to exclude superpositions incompatible with the corporeal nature of X. And thus another long-standing conundrum of quantum theory has been resolved.

The most profoundly significant fact of all, however, is that *the effect of vertical causation emanating from a corporeal object X is by no means limited to the immediate vicinity of X, but can in principle encompass all of space!* And herein indeed resides the wonder of Bell's theorem,[13] which has caused such consternation among physicists. Let me recall the salient fact as illustrated by the example of the twin photons in a state of "parallel polarization," traveling respectively to points A and B, perhaps millions of miles apart. The fact is that a measurement which determines the polarization of the photon at A *instantly* determines the polarization of its twin at B as well. Now, what shocks physicists in this scenario is the fact that *horizontal* causality is categorically incapable of accounting for this effect—which however signifies simply that the prodigy constitutes perforce an effect of *vertical* causation. Bell's theorem affirming the non-existence of "local" objects thus entails not only the "ubiquity" of vertical causation, but its well-nigh miraculous efficacy as well: for not only does VC act instantaneously, but *its effect is not diminished by spatial separation.*

---

12. I am referring to the so-called "Schrödinger paradox." See *Ancient Wisdom and Modern Misconceptions*, ch. 1.

13. See chapter 2, 23–25.

From a metaphysical point of view, that well-nigh miraculous efficacy is implied by the fact that vertical causality operates *instantaneously*; for as we have noted at the outset, this situates the origin of that causality at the highest level of the cosmic hierarchy: at the Apex of the integral cosmos, one can say, which transcends not only the bound of time, but consequently the bound of space as well. Vertical causality proves thus to be not only "higher" but incomparably more powerful than the modes of causality hitherto known to physics, which actually stem from the opposite direction: that is, from the subcorporeal domain.[14]

14. It must not be forgotten, however, that even though horizontal causality derives from a subcorporeal plane, it is yet "activated" by vertical causality, as is clearly evident in the instance of quantum measurement.

4

Three Vertical
Powers of the Soul

The soul is partly in eternity, and partly in time.

PLATO

This brings to a close our cycle of reflections centered upon quantum physics. As we have come to see, the resolution of the quantum enigma hinges upon two primary distinctions: the *ontological* discernment between the *corporeal* and the *physical* domains, and the *etiological* between *horizontal* and *vertical* causation. But whereas the notion of corporeal being constitutes a basic conception of traditional philosophy, it appears that the existence of vertical causality has remained essentially unrecognized and unexplored.

It is time, I believe, to remedy this neglect: the present crisis demands no less. Having been subjected to what might be termed "the tyranny of horizontal causation" since the onset of the Enlightenment, it is high time to realize that all the causalities known to physics prove in fact to be *secondary*, with a sphere of operation restricted to the lower extremities of the integral cosmos, whereas the primary mode of causation—whose sphere of action extends through the length and breadth of the cosmos, from its Apex down to a particle of dust—proves to be inexorably *vertical*. The moment has arrived, it seems to me, for this decisive fact to be brought into the light of day: the defeat of scientistic materialism—the restoration of our collective sanity!—appears to demand nothing less.

Given that, among natural functions, human intelligence may be the most closely connected to "vertical" causality, let us now shift our attention, from fundamental physics to the opposite end of the *scala naturae*, to investigate the active and cognitive faculties of mankind, in the expectation that these will prove in fact to be *vertical*, that is to say, supratemporal in their mode of action. It turns out that not only God, but man too has a certain "access" to the *nunc stans*: the elusive "now that stands," which as we have noted, constitutes the central Point and Apex of the integral cosmos.

∽

Inasmuch as we shall be dealing with "powers of the soul," it is needful, first of all, to consider—following centuries of oblivion—what exactly is meant by a "soul." Recalling the Aristotelian distinction between *morphe* and *hyle* ("form" and "matter"), let us note that a corporeal entity is what it is by virtue of its "formal" component, known as a "substantial form." Thus, in the absence of a substantial form, that putative entity *has no* "what," which of course entails that like the so-called fundamental particles of quantum physics, it does not actually exist as an entity, as a "thing." But if the "what" of an entity is specified by its substantial form, it is that form which determines whether the entity is animate or inanimate. Thus, in the case of an animal, that form is called an *anima* or *soul*, and in that of man, it is—for good reason—termed a *rational* soul. After death, in any case, when the soul has separated from the body, what remains of the body is no longer, strictly speaking, an entity, but what is termed a "mixture": a composite of inanimate substances, which as such is prone to decompose.

So much by way of recounting the most basic metaphysical conceptions. The notion we are about to introduce, on the other hand, pertains to what may perhaps be termed the deepest level of the Thomistic ontology. If it be the substantial form that founds a being (animate or inanimate), we now ask what it is that founds the substantial form itself: and that is what St. Thomas refers to as *the act of being*. As the Master himself explains: "The act-of-being is the most intimate element in anything, and the most profound element in all things, because it is like a form in regard to all that is in the thing."[1] The act-of-being proves thus to be none other than the cosmogenetic Act itself, viewed in relation to a specific being. And that act-of-being, moreover, bestows not only *being*, but also *a power to act with an efficacy of its own*. As Etienne Gilson observes magnificently:

> The universe, as represented by St. Thomas, is not a mass of inert bodies passively moved by a force which passes through them, but a collection of active beings each enjoying an efficacy delegated to it by God along with actual being.[2]

This brings us to a crucial point: on every level, that "efficacy delegated by God" entails a capacity, on the part of created beings, to achieve all manner of effects by way of *vertical* causation—beginning with the rudimentary examples pertaining to the inanimate realm previously cited in the context of quantum theory. Turning now to the opposite end of the *scala naturae*, namely to the anthropic sphere, one sees that the prime example of vertical causation proves to be precisely what is traditionally termed "free will": for what else does the adjective "free" signify in this context than the capacity to act—not as a marionette, through the action of external causes, but indeed "from within." An act is "free," therefore, by virtue of the fact that it is not effected by a chain of external causes, but by the soul, the *anima* which acts from within, and hence by way of vertical causation.[3]

Moreover, in addition to "active" powers delegated by God, man is endowed with "cognitive" powers as well; and here too one finds that "verticality" in the sense of the "supra-temporal" proves to be key: for it turns out, as we shall see, that both visual and intellectual perception (the kind manifested, for instance, in understanding the proof of a mathematical theorem) demand a *supra-temporal* act. Now, to be "supra-temporal" means to be situated in the *nunc stans*:

---

1. *Summa Theologiae* I, 8, 1.
2. *The Christian Philosophy of St. Thomas Aquinas* (University of Notre Dame Press, 1994), 183.
3. The theoretical possibility of constraint "from above" by way of vertical causation has already been ruled out, and is in any case not normally under consideration when one speaks of "free will."

for between the seeming "now that moves" and the "now that stands" there is no middle term. Both of the aforesaid cognitive faculties presuppose therefore a capacity to "access" the *nunc stans*: to "step out of time," as it were. And that transcendence of time—of the temporal condition, if you will—has served from the start as the defining characteristic of the "vertical" in the sense we have made our own. In a word, the concept of "verticality" applies not only to causation, but to cognition as well.

I will point out in passing that if every corporeal object gives rise to acts of vertical causality—as we have shown—it should come as no surprise that this capacity to activate VC increases as we ascend from the inorganic to the organic domain, and attains its zenith in man, the *anthropos*.[4] It should moreover be noted that between the extremes of the inorganic and the anthropic there must exist a plethora of "vertical" effects which a higher kind of science could presumably discover and put to good use, but which will remain undiscovered until it dawns upon the scientific community that causality exists actually in *two* modes: horizontal *and* vertical. When it comes to the ontologically higher domains, our sciences—as presently conceived—may actually be losing the better half of the picture. For those capable, on the other hand, of thinking "outside the box," the opportunities for the discovery of deeper and more powerful sciences appear to be vast.

Free Will as Vertical Causality

The connection between "free will" and vertical causation came to light abruptly in 1998 when a mathematician named William Dembski published a remarkable theorem.[5] Having introduced the decisive concept of "complex specified information" or CSI, Dembski stunned the scientific world by proving—with complete mathematical rigor—that *no physical process, be it deterministic, random or*

---

4. It is to be understood that we are speaking of what may be termed the "sub-angelic" realm.

5. *The Design Inference* (Cambridge University Press, 1998).

stochastic,[6] *can produce CSI.* But this means, in our terminology, that what has thus been disqualified from producing CSI is none other than *horizontal* causality! Wherever, therefore, we encounter the production of CSI, we have documented an act of *vertical* causation.

Now it appears that humans produce CSI almost incessantly; I myself, for instance, am apparently doing so at this very moment by writing these lines. And we take it in our stride: we see nothing remotely exceptional or astounding in these quotidian acts. Little do we realize that the metaphysical implications of this capacity are profound in the extreme, to the point that an inkling, even, of what actually transpires would in fact suffice to disqualify the contemporary Weltanschauung irrevocably: for the intervention of vertical causation actually entails a certain "access" on the part of man to the *nunc stans*, that elusive "now" that is said to "stand still," in which, according to Meister Eckhart, "*God creates the world and all things.*"

I should add that, in point of mathematical rigor, the aforesaid argument is yet incomplete: for inasmuch as we have access to an immense store of CSI—e.g., in the form of memory—it remains to show that the CSI we are said to "produce" (as I am doing right now, say, by composing this book) is not already "given" in that store. But whereas I fully acknowledge the logical force of this objection, I find it quite inconceivable that a chain of horizontal causation could take us—presumably by algorithmic means—from such "given CSI" to the "produced."[7] And I would add that by the time we recognize the verticality of visual perception and the non-algorithmic nature of mathematical proof—the subjects of the next two sections—there will be no more need, in this context, for information-theoretic argument. What I find remarkable is not that this kind of reasoning can take us only so far, but rather that a science

6. A "stochastic" process is partly deterministic and partly random, as in the case of Brownian motion.

7. Of course the question remains how the "given CSI" itself was produced. And here again Dembski's theorem implies that somewhere along the line an act of vertical causation *must have* intervened.

which excludes all essence from its purview can in fact arrive at a conclusion as powerful as Dembski's theorem.

The Verticality of Visual Perception

It has been assumed for centuries that the eye is in effect a camera, and that what we perceive is based upon a retinal image. One is quite certain, moreover, not just that this is the only reasonable way to account for visual perception, but that this "image theory" has been corroborated by an abundance of evidence, beginning presumably with the fact that spectacles affect vision in keeping with that paradigm. What we are not told, on the other hand, is that in the 40's of the last century, a cognitive psychologist at Cornell University, named James Gibson, serendipitously uncovered facts which *rigorously disqualify this visual-image theory*, and that in the course of three subsequent decades of empirical research he succeeded in replacing that now discredited paradigm by one which does square with the empirical facts. Having dealt elsewhere[8] and at considerable length with this epochal discovery, it will suffice to highlight the main findings which both reveal and establish the supra-temporal nature of visual perception.

According to Gibson, what we perceive visually is not an image—be it retinal, cerebral, or mental—but so-called *invariants* given in what he terms *ambient*—as distinguished from *radiant*—light. By "ambient" light he means light reflected from the environment, which Gibson conceives, not in "physical," but in what he refers to as "ecological" terms. To make a long story short: Gibson's use of the term "ecological" proves ultimately tantamount to what I term *corporeal*, the point being that Gibson's "environment" owns not only quantitative attributes, but *qualities* as well. What then are the "invariants" we are said to "pick up" in the act of visual perception? Gibson, to be sure, speaks of these in his own "research-based" terms; yet in light of traditional metaphysics, what actually stands at issue are none other than *forms*. And let us note at once: if what we "pick up" in the act of visual perception are indeed forms, then—

8. *Science & Myth*, ch. 4.

and then only!—is it possible to perceive, not simply an image or phantasm, but the very objects: that is to say, *the external world itself*. For in that case we perceive—not a mere image or *effect* of that world—but the very forms that constitute its reality.

Gibson's discovery, as noted before, amounts thus to *a scientific refutation of the Cartesian doctrine*: specifically its epistemology, which affirms that the object of perception constitutes a mere phantasm or "thing of the mind." Even as Heisenberg's physics has demonstrated that there exists actually no such thing as a Cartesian *res extensa*, so has Gibson's discovery toppled the second pillar of the Cartesian edifice: the misbegotten notion of *res cogitans*. The amazing fact—which Gibson himself clearly recognized—is that his so-called "ecological" theory of visual perception has validated the immemorial premise that we do actually "look out" upon the world, which thus proves to be—not the world as conceived or imagined by the physicist—but none other than what we have termed the *corporeal*.

It is essential to recognize that this radical shift in our understanding of *what* we actually perceive necessitates a corresponding change in our conception of how that perception is effected. What needs above all to be understood is that so long as the faculties of perception are themselves a mere aggregate or "sum of parts," a "pick-up" of *forms* is simply inconceivable. So long, therefore, as one conceives of the percipient in what might be referred to as "post-Enlightenment" terms, an understanding of perception proves thus to be impossible: that very premise suffices to render it such. And amazingly, as time went on, Gibson the quintessential empiricist came to realize this ontological fact with ever greater clarity: his experimental findings actually demand nothing less. It turns out that one cannot in fact understand visual perception simply by looking at the retina or at the behavior of neurons in affected parts of the brain. This is not to say, of course, that these processes have nothing to do with visual perception; the point, rather, is that *they are part of a process which in truth is more than the sum of its parts*. And it came to pass that Gibson—this genius of an empiricist—came, by gradual and meticulous steps, to understand that the mystery of perception resides precisely in this "more." It remains only to point out that this "more" is finally none other than what is traditionally termed a "soul."

The power of visual perception derives thus, in the final count, from the *soul*. And inasmuch as the soul is united to the body as its substantial form, what to the neuro-scientist appears as a vast ensemble of neuronal activity *constitutes in reality a single event, a single act of the living and sentient organism*. The point is simple: if perception were merely a matter of neuronal firings, we would need a homunculus—a little man within the brain—to "read" these events—which is of course absurd. It should therefore come as no surprise when Sir Francis Crick (of DNA fame) informs us that "*we can see how the brain takes the picture apart, but we do not yet see how it puts it together*"[9]—the point being that the brain itself *cannot* in fact "put it together" at all: it takes the *soul* to accomplish that prodigy. And the reason, moreover, why it *can* do so resides in the ontological fact that *the soul is not subject to the bounds of space.* Let us note what this entails: it is by virtue of the resultant "ubiquity" that the soul can actually be present to each cell in the body—not as some minute fragment of itself—but in its undivided and undiminished entirety.[10]

Yet it turns out that even this marvelous capacity—this seemingly miraculous ability on the part of the soul to transcend spatial bounds—does not yet suffice: for it happens that the prodigy of visual perception requires a comparable transcendence of *temporal bounds* as well! And this too came to light in the course of Gibson's experiments, culminating in the recognition that we perceive motion, not "moment by moment," but the only way motion *can* in fact be perceived: *all at once*! Yet, amazing as this fact may be, it is hardly surprising: for if in fact we did perceive "moment by moment," we would in principle fare no better than a camera, which is able to "see" merely a succession of images while the motion itself remains invisible.

9. *The Astonishing Hypothesis* (New York: Simon & Schuster, 1995), 159.

10. Once one catches so much as a glimpse of what the transcendence of space—the existence of the intermediary domain—actually entails, one's outlook regarding contemporary science will never be the same.

I would emphasize that Gibson's arguments are both subtle and fully rigorous once the point has been grasped, and confirm unequivocally that visual perception constitutes indeed a *vertical* act. Plato was right: so far from being confined to the temporal realm, the soul does in truth *have access to eternity.*

The Verticality of Intellect

Once it had been assumed that the external world of *res extensae* constitutes a single gigantic mechanism, it did not take long for the enlightened ones to draw the conclusion that man too is basically a mechanism. And this entails that his so-called intellectual capacities must likewise be the result of some—presumably cerebral—machinery. Around the fateful year 1900, moreover, the basic component of that hypothesized mechanism—the so-called neuron—was identified by a Spanish biologist named Ramón y Cajal; and that discovery, as one might surmise, gave rise to a worldwide brain-research enterprise designed to ascertain the structure and *modus operandi* of that horrendously complex "machine" made up of neurons: close to 100 billion in all.

Around the year 1936, moreover, another fundamental breakthrough occurred, which soon proved to be related. It happened when a mathematician, named Alan Turing, posed the question whether mathematical reasoning as such could, in principle, be carried out by a "machine" or mechanism of some sort. Now the kind of "reasoning" Turing had in mind has since been termed *algorithmic*; and what he did—to the amazement of the mathematical world—was to construct what has ever since been termed a Turing machine: a device, existing "on paper" if you will, capable in principle of executing every conceivable algorithm by means of a corresponding "program" inscribed in the "software" part of the machine. The fact is that Turing discovered the universal prototype of which every computer in the world constitutes a partial embodiment.

In the wake of this epochal discovery it came to be widely assumed that the human brain functions—at least in part—as a computer, and that human intelligence is consequently *algorithmic*.

There can be little doubt, moreover, that this has been the reigning paradigm in the pertinent fields of scientific endeavor ever since the discovery of the Turing machine: that to this day, in fact, it constitutes the underlying premise upon which our scientific understanding of "human intelligence" is based. It may therefore come as a shock to many that this putatively "scientific" tenet turns out to be not only questionable, but *has in fact been disproved with mathematical rigor.* That is what I wish now to explain as briefly as I can.

The argument is based upon a stupendous theorem, proved in 1933 by a 25-year-old mathematician named Kurt Gödel, which affirms that given a set of mathematical axioms (extensive enough to encompass arithmetical propositions), there must exist a proposition which is *true* but *unprovable* in that system. The proof of Gödel's theorem is based upon the amazing fact that not only arithmetical propositions, but all possible proofs of such within a given axiom system can be "ordered": that is to say, indexed by the natural numbers 1, 2, 3... Now this is the part of the proof which is both technical and difficult in the extreme, whereas what remains—though highly ingenious—turns out to be rather simple. Here then is that second part, which concludes Gödel's argument:

By virtue of Part I, we may assume that there exists a function $P(m,n)$, defined for all natural numbers m and n, such that, for every m, $P(m,n)$ is a propositional function of n (an algebraic statement depending on n, which may be true or false) and a function $\Pi(k)$ which orders all mathematical proofs in the given axiom system.

We now define the following propositional function: "There exists no k such that $\Pi(k)$ proves $P(w,w)$." Since our enumeration $P(m,n)$ of arithmetical propositions is complete, there must exist a natural number s such that $P(s,n)$ is the aforesaid function. Now consider the proposition $P(s,s)$: the first thing to note is that this proposition is unprovable (since our construction entails that "there exists no k such that $\Pi(k)$ proves $P(s,s)$");[11] and the second is that $P(s,s)$ is true: for indeed there exists no k such that $\Pi(k)$ proves $P(s,s)$.

---

11. The reader will note that the propositional functions $P(k,k)$ and $P(s,s)$ are evidently one and the same.

And this is how Gödel proved the existence of true but unprovable propositions!

The question, now, is whether this theorem has been proved by way of an algorithm or not. It is always possible, of course, to claim that an algorithm of some kind has unwittingly played out in the process of arriving at a given conclusion; but as Roger Penrose observes, the algorithms used in mathematics are well known and communicable, and it is evident in the case of Gödel's theorem that no such has come into play. In a word, the intelligence which enabled us to understand the proof in question is manifestly non-algorithmic. "When we convince ourselves of the validity of Gödel's theorem," Penrose goes on to say, "we not only 'see' it, but in so doing we reveal the very non-algorithmic nature of the 'seeing' process itself."[12] Now, we concur with this statement wholeheartedly—except for one word: we must insist that this "seeing" is not in fact a "process," but a *vertical* and therefore *instantaneous* act. As the expression goes, it is manifestly a question of "seeing the point"—and a "point" is to be seen "all at once" or not at all.

One should add that precisely the same actually holds true when a theorem is supposedly proved by an algorithm: for it is actually not the algorithm that proves the theorem, but the person who "sees" that it does. Strictly speaking, a formal proof of a mathematical theorem can do no more than elicit, in those who are qualified, a perception of its validity. The fact that an argument or chain of reasoning constitutes a proof by virtue of meeting appropriate criteria of validity is of course undeniable—but that does not obviate the necessity of "seeing the point." Thus, in the final count, science is indeed "*nothing but perception*," as Plato noted long ago. In the end—when the work has been accomplished and the quest attained its goal—that's what it reduces to. And that consummation, let us add, is achieved—not by the rational faculty, which is discursive and operates in time—but by the *intellect*, properly so called, which does *not* operate in time, but in what has been termed the *nunc stans*. For the intellect is indeed the "eye of the soul" by which we *see*: the "part," as Plato says, which "pertains to eternity."

---

12. *The Emperor's New Mind* (Oxford University Press, 1989), 418.

5

The War on Design

Since the seventeenth century, Western civilization has been subject to the spell of a new and supposedly "scientific" Weltanschauung, initiated by Galileo, Descartes and Newton. From the publication of Newton's *Principia* in 1687 to the discovery of quantum physics in the early twentieth century, it was assumed by the pundits of the Enlightenment that, at bottom, the universe constitutes a gigantic "clockwork," in which the disposition of the parts determines—with mathematical precision!—the movement of the whole. And even in the face of the quantum facts, that paradigm was not actually discarded, but merely modified. To this day one is prone to conceive of the universe basically as a "clockwork," howbeit one which no longer functions with absolute precision: one could say that in addition to rigid cogwheels, it now comprises some "wobbly" components as well, which in effect play the role of "dice." The larger picture, thus, has scarcely changed at all: now as before, Nature is perceived, on scientific authority, as constituting precisely what Whitehead referred to as "a dull affair": merely "the hurrying of material, endlessly, meaninglessly."[1]

With the appearance of what we have termed "vertical causation," however, the picture has radically changed. I need hardly recount how, beginning with the quantum measurement problem, vertical causation has come into view time and again, profoundly affecting the entire spectrum of scientific domains—from physics to cognitive psychology—touching even, if you will, upon the mathematical sciences.

---

1. *Science and the Modern World* (New York: Macmillan, 1953), 54.

In light of these findings—and this is the first major point I wish now to convey—it emerges that our natural sciences have presently reached a stage at which the next round of foundational discovery may very well hinge upon a recognition of vertical causality. I say "foundational," because it is of course always possible to investigate this or that phenomenon along already established lines, and in so doing reap whatever technological or other benefits may ensue. Obviously, however, I am referring to something quite different: to the question, for instance, how the mysterious and hitherto inexplicable "epigenome" fits into genetics as presently conceived, or what neuronal structures can and cannot accomplish by way of facilitating thought, perception, memory and the like.[2] If not perhaps the first, then most assuredly the second question requires that we bring the concept of vertical causation into play. I surmise that when it comes to research of a truly foundational kind, we are approaching the end of what can in principle be understood on the basis of horizontal causality alone, and that much of what presently impedes progress at the frontiers of scientific inquiry may prove, ultimately, to be an effect of VC. What is called for, I maintain, is a vastly deepened understanding of Nature, based upon the recognition that horizontal causality, so far from standing alone, is perforce complemented in the final count by vertical modes of causation. It is high time, I would argue, to jettison our Galilean, Cartesian, and Newtonian assumptions and become philosophically literate once again.

Inasmuch as vertical causation presents itself in numerous modes, some fundamental distinctions need now to be made. The primary dichotomy stems from the fundamental recognition touched upon earlier: the fact, namely, that *the act of being* bestows upon creatures not only existence by way of a substantial form, but also an efficacy,

---

2. I have dealt with this question in a general way in "Neurons and Mind." See *Science and Myth*.

a certain power to act. To be precise, every corporeal entity is endowed with a capacity to act by way of vertical causation; and inasmuch as this power pertains to the substantial form, we may refer to it as *substantial* VC. It is also needful, however, to recognize a higher mode of vertical causality, which does not emanate from a substantial form, but can in fact *give rise to* substantial forms, a mode which we may consequently refer to as *creative*. And this brings us finally to the subject of the present chapter: the notion of *design*. What do we mean by this term? One is prone to say that "design" is simply an effect of creative VC; but this is far too broad to be of much use: for what then, in the universe, would *not* be an instance of design? To be of interest, the concept should be restricted to what in fact *cannot* be produced by "the hurrying of material, endlessly, meaninglessly." There are then, first of all, two instances of design which prove to be of special interest, one terrestrial and the other cosmic: *speciation* namely, and a marvelous order pertaining to the cosmos at large, which we term *immobility*, a concept that will emerge in the course of our inquiry.

Which brings me finally to the subject of the present chapter: "The War on Design." My first contention should hardly come as a surprise: I charge that the Darwinist claim, so far from constituting a scientific hypothesis supported by empirical evidence, proves to be in truth an *ideological* tenet, based upon the *a priori* denial of design in the form of speciation.[3] It is my second claim, rather, that may cause astonishment: I shall contend that even as Darwinism rests upon the denial of design in the origin of species, relativistic physics at large is based upon the *a priori* rejection of design in the form of *immobility*. Einsteinian physics proves thus to be a kind of Darwinism on a cosmic scale; and turns out in the end—to the surprise and consternation of many—to be likewise untenable.

---

3. It is safe to say that with the discovery of DNA around the middle of the last century Darwinism was in effect disqualified as a scientific theory. With the publication moreover of Dembski's 1998 theorem regarding "complex specified information" it has been rigorously disproved on mathematical grounds, and thus reduced from a bona-fide scientific hypothesis to the status of a sociological phenomenon.

The Theoretical Basis of Einsteinian Physics

Let us begin by reflecting upon Einstein's 1905 paper, which inaugurates his so-called "special" theory of relativity.[4] The ostensible mission of that article—its accomplishment one might say—was to impose a condition upon physics referred to as the Principle of Relativity. But what is it, precisely, that motivated Albert Einstein to modify the classical equations, to render them "relativistic"? Why *should* the laws of physics be "invariant" in that specific sense? Let us see how Einstein himself responds to this question.

In the survey of his theory, special plus general, published under the title *The Meaning of Relativity*,[5] Einstein begins by recalling the basic facts of analytic geometry, starting with the concept of a Cartesian coordinate system. For the sake of concreteness, let's suppose for the moment that we are dealing with the Euclidean plane in which a point O (termed "the origin") has been specified. A Cartesian coordinate system consists then of two mutually perpendicular and oriented lines through O. With every point P in the plane one can now associate a pair of coordinates (x_1, x_2), defined by the perpendicular projections of P onto the corresponding axes.[6] It follows—by the venerable Pythagorean theorem[7] no less—that the square of the distance OP equals $x_1^2 + x_2^2$. What is crucial here is the fact that this relation—this "law"—holds in *every* Cartesian coordinate system, that it is thus *"invariant."*

Now, simple and elementary as these considerations may be, they can serve admirably as a point of departure for an introduction to Einsteinian physics. Getting back to our example: let us note that a coordinate system effects a transition from a *geometric* to an *analytical* structure, which obviously depends upon the coordinate system we happen to choose. The problem, then, is to discover what, in a given representation, is independent of that choice: is thus "geomet-

---

4. As distinguished from his "general" theory, published in 1917.

5. Princeton University Press, 1955.

6. To be precise: If Q_i denotes the projection of P onto the ith axis, we define x_i to be the distance (positive or negative) from O to Q_i.

7. "The sum of the squares of the sides of a right triangle equals the square of the hypotenuse."

rical" like the expression $x_1{}^2 + x_2{}^2$. It is needful, in other words, to distinguish the "non-geometrical" elements introduced by this construction from properties indigenous to the Euclidean space: and this is where the all-important notion of *invariance* comes into play. In the case of Cartesian coordinates in the Euclidean plane, the term $x_1{}^2 + x_2{}^2$ is a prime example of an invariant: as we have noted, it equals the length squared of the line segment OP.

The key conception of Einsteinian physics can now be explained: for it happens that Albert Einstein was fascinated by geometry, and conceived of physics in basically geometric terms. What now takes the place of the Euclidean plane is the locus of all "points in space" and "moments in time," which has since come to be known as the *space-time continuum*. Einstein's objective—his momentous idea— was to reduce physics in effect to a geometry on this 4-dimensional manifold. But of course, Einstein the quintessential physicist conceived of that space-time, not as a mathematical abstraction, but— true to Lord Kelvin's definition of physics as "the science of measurement"—as based upon mensuration.

What then constitutes an Einsteinian "coordinate system"? The question reduces to this: Given a point P in space-time, how can one associate an ordered set of four real numbers (x_1, x_2, x_3, x_4) with that point? One can do so, in principle, by means of a reference *frame* K, which we may picture as consisting of three mutually perpendicular rods emanating from a point O. It is apparent that such a frame enables us "in principle" to assign four coordinates to every "point" P in space-time: three spatial coordinates (x_1, x_2, x_3) namely, plus a "time-coordinate" t as measured by a clock stationary with respect to K.

The next step in the construction of Einsteinian "space-time" geometry is to define the analog of "distance": i.e., to specify what plays the role of $x_1{}^2 + x_2{}^2$ in the Euclidean plane. And for good mathematical reasons, Einstein chose the quadratic form $x_1{}^2 + x_2{}^2 + x_3{}^2 - c^2 t^2$, where c denotes the speed of light. In the first place, since it obviously makes no sense to add, say, *seconds* to *meters*, it is necessary to multiply t by a *velocity* to obtain a *distance*. But why choose the light velocity c? And again, for good reasons: apart from the fact that there are grounds to suppose that c constitutes a universal constant, it happens that coordinate transformations which preserve the given quadratic form—the so-called Lorentz transformations—preserve the Maxwell equations of electromagnetism as well. By this choice Einstein has therefore taken the decisive step in the construction of a physics in which the phenomena of electromagnetism can be viewed in geometric terms. One thing more, however, needs to be done, and that is to specify the actual reference frames—the so-called *inertial* frames—which in this space-time geometry will play the role of a Cartesian coordinate system: then only does the Einsteinian space-time acquire a physical sense, and thus engender predictions which can actually be put to the test.

How then does Einstein define the class of *inertial frames* K? He does so in his 1905 debut by what he terms "*the principle of special relativity*,"[8] which asserts that *if K is inertial and K' moves uniformly and without rotation with respect to K, then K' is likewise inertial.* One consequently needs but to identify a single inertial frame K_0 to determine the entire class.

Let us suppose now that we have identified such a "first" reference frame K_0, and that the classical (i.e., pre-relativistic and pre-quantum) equations of physics hold in K_0. The question, now, is whether they hold likewise in every other inertial reference frame K. If so, then classical physics satisfies Einstein's principle of special relativity; and of course: if not, it doesn't. To resolve this issue we need first of all to recall that the classical equations of physics divide into two groups: the equations of mechanics, which go back to Sir Isaac Newton's *Principia*, published in 1687, and the equations of electromagnetism, formulated 178 years later by Clerk Maxwell. Now we know from the start that the equations of electromagnetism do satisfy Einstein's principle of special relativity, by the fact that they are Lorentz invariant. As we have pointed out, the Einsteinian geometry

---

8. The adjective "special" does not appear in the 1905 paper, but was added after the so-called "general theory of relativity" appeared.

is actually "tailor-made" to render the Maxwell equations "geometrical"! The real test of Einsteinian relativity, therefore, comes from the side of mechanics: do these classical Newtonian equations satisfy Einstein's Principle or do they not? And it is obvious, by the fact that these equations are *not* Lorentz invariant, that indeed they do not.

To summarize up to this point: Albert Einstein has constructed a "relativistic" physics, conceived in terms of a space-time geometry, which is compatible with the Maxwell theory of electromagnetism but *not* with the Newtonian mechanics. Now this leaves him, obviously, with two options: to reject his so-called "special theory of relativity" on the grounds that it does not square with the equations of mechanics, or to alter these equations—to render them "relativistic" by fiat as it were—to save his theory. And needless to say, Einstein chose the second course: the Procrustean option, his critics might say.

Two possibilities remain: either Einstein is right and the equations of classical mechanics need indeed to be revised, or the equations of classical mechanics are correct as they stand, and it is actually his "relativistic" mechanics that proves to be false. How, then, does Einstein argue his case: on what grounds does he justify his theory? To answer this question we turn now to his original 1905 paper, published in the *Annalen der Physik*—under the rather unassuming title *"On the electrodynamics of moving bodies"*—which marks the birth of "relativistic" physics, to see how Einstein himself justified his revolutionary proposal.

As might be expected, he begins by recounting experiments pertaining to the domain of *electromagnetism* to exhibit observable phenomena which do "depend only on relative motion," that is to say, satisfy his stipulated Principle of Relativity.[9] But what about the "other half" of classical physics: the equations of mechanics? Einstein gives a very brief (and interesting!) answer to this question.

9. The adjective "special" was introduced later, as noted above.

Having alluded—in the opening paragraph of his paper—to certain electromagnetic phenomena (which, as we have noted, comply with his Principle), he begins the second paragraph as follows: "Examples of this sort," he writes, "together with the unsuccessful attempts to discover any motion of the Earth relative to the 'light medium,' suggest that the phenomena of electrodynamics *as well as of mechanics* [my italics] possess no properties corresponding to the idea of absolute rest. They suggest rather that, as has already been shown to the first order of small quantities, the same laws of electrodynamics and optics will be valid for all frames of reference for which the equations of mechanics hold good. We will raise this conjecture (hereafter referred to as the 'Principle of Relativity') to the status of a postulate."

The reasoning here is astonishing. Let us first of all consider Einstein's allusion to the Michelson-Morley experiment of 1887, which, as one knows, was designed to detect and measure the postulated orbital velocity of the Earth around the Sun (said to be around 30 km/sec), but proved "unsuccessful" inasmuch as no such velocity was found. On what basis therefore, let us ask, does Einstein rule out the theoretical possibility that the experiment may actually have proved that in fact *there is no* such "orbital" velocity, as the Michelson-Morley finding appears to attest? After all, given that the question pertains to physical science *on its most fundamental level*, it would seem that no conceptual possibility—no matter how apparently improbable—should be ruled out simply "by a wave of the hand"! And as a matter of fact: to imply that a "uniform motion without rotation" is not detectable is to beg the very question which stands at issue: namely, whether or not the Einsteinian Principle of Relativity is true.

What I find still more surprising, however, is Einstein's claim that empirical findings "suggest that the phenomena of electrodynamics *as well as of mechanics*" conform to his postulate: for whereas, in the case of electrodynamics, the property in question follows mathematically from the fact that Maxwell's equations for the electromagnetic field are in fact Lorentz invariant, the opposite holds true for the classical equations of mechanics. For unlike electrodynamics, classical mechanics happen *not* to be Lorentz invariant; and whereas it was consequently a foregone conclusion that "the phenomena of electrodynamics" conform to Einstein's Principle, the opposite holds true in the case of mechanics. In other words, even as the phenomena of electrodynamics *predictably* obey the Principle of Relativity, so on the strength of classical physics "the phenomena of mechanics" *predictably* do not. Now to be sure, Einstein was well aware of the fact that the classical equations of mechanics do *not* obey his Principle—which is after all the reason he felt obliged to alter them, to render them "relativistic." My point is that this fateful step was, in the final count, authorized by nothing more substantial than the failure of the Michelson-Morley experiment to detect the postulated—but never yet observed!—"orbital" velocity of the Earth.

There is thus no complete—let alone compelling—argument to justify the shift from classical to relativistic physics. Einstein's pivotal allusion to the Michelson-Morley experiment has no doubt a powerful *psychological* efficacy within the scientific community, but actually carries no weight: given that the experiment was designed to detect and measure—for the very first time—a conjectured velocity, its failure to confirm that hypothetical motion hardly disproves the validity of classical mechanics!

Moreover, there is nothing in any way illogical, incongruous, or scientifically objectionable in the fact that the equations governing mechanical phenomena and those which describe electromagnetic fields should be invariant under different groups (Galilean and Lorentz, respectively). It could in fact be argued quite cogently that in view of the radically different nature of these respective domains, such a discrepancy is rather to be expected. In any case, there appears to be no bona-fide argument which would exclude that possibility, and Einstein's above-cited reference to "the phenomena of mechanics" most certainly doesn't alter this fact.

Meanwhile it is a mathematical fact that, so far from satisfying Einstein's Principle of Relativity, the equations of classical physics—mechanics plus electromagnetism—actually entail the very opposite: they imply, namely, that if the equations of mechanics *and* of electromagnetism both hold in two reference frames K_0 and K, then K is in fact *stationary* with respect to K_0. Instead of the Einsteinian

Principle of Relativity, we actually have here a Principle of *Immobility*—and not as a conjecture in conflict with the equations of mechanics, but as a *theorem of classical physics*. The fact is that pre-Einsteinian physics implies the very opposite of Einstein's postulate: in place of an ensemble of "inertial" reference frames in uniform motion with respect to each other, in which none can be singled out on physical grounds, one finds that *physics itself defines a state of absolute rest.*

So far as I know, neither Albert Einstein nor any post-Einsteinian physicist of repute has ever so much as mentioned this remarkable fact, let alone explored its implications. No one among the *avant-garde* physicists appears to have seriously entertained the possibility that *the equations of classical mechanics may actually be correct!* In place of a Principle of Immobility corroborated empirically for well over half a century,[10] they have opted for a Principle of Relativity for which there is actually no empirical validation at all: that *conjectured* Principle takes precedence, in their mind, over three centuries of scientific verification![11] But why? On what grounds does Einstein justify his rejection of classical mechanics? When and where, exactly, did it fail? Does he have nothing more cogent to offer in that regard than the reputed "failure" of the Michelson-Morley experiment?

I contend that the Einsteinian preference for the Principle of Relativity is based in the final count—not on scientific or empirical grounds—but on *ideological* premises. The fact is that the existence of *immobile* reference frames is closely tied to geocentrism, which constitutes—unmistakably!—an instance of *design*. Considering then that "design" implicates a Designer, it is hardly surprising that geocentrism has long been taboo to the scientific elite; for as Richard Lewontin, speaking for the scientific community at large, apprises us: "*We cannot allow a Divine Foot in the Door.*"

10. Since 1865 in fact, when Clerk Maxwell wrote down the equations of the electromagnetic field.

11. The equations of classical mechanics, which Einstein rejected, have been in use since 1687.

ॐ

Classical physics, by virtue of what we have termed the Principle of Immobility, affirms the existence of "*stationary*" reference frames: frames K, namely, in which the classical equations of mechanics and of electromagnetism both hold. And this brings us to the crucial question: what about *geocentric* reference frames (frames at rest with respect to the Earth): are these in fact stationary, or are they not? If they are, this would mean that *classical physics entails geocentrism!*

What evidently stands in the way of this conclusion is the seemingly sacrosanct tenet that the Earth rotates around its polar axis: every 24 hours, to be exact. One needs therefore to ask oneself whether this reputed fact has been rigorously established by scientific means. Of course, if the question were asked, the overwhelming majority of respondents—from laymen to astrophysicists—would, without a moment's hesitation, answer in the affirmative. Yet it happens that this virtually unanimous verdict proves to be incorrect: for it follows, by what is termed *Mach's Principle*, that it is not in fact possible to ascertain by empirical means whether it is the Earth that rotates while the cosmos at large stands still, or whether, on the contrary, it is the cosmos at large that rotates diurnally around a stationary Earth.

This is all we need to know: it permits us to affirm without fear of contradiction, based squarely upon classical physics, that *geocentric reference frames are stationary.* And thus one arrives at what is in effect the pre-Copernican cosmography, which conceives the Earth as an immobile sphere situated at the center of the universe, which consequently revolves diurnally around the Earth's polar axis. It appears that Einstein's 1905 Principle of Relativity, so far from being necessitated on scientific grounds, was based on an *a priori* rejection of what I have termed the Principle of Immobility, and thus of classical physics *per se*, which entails that Principle. The modifications imposed upon the equations of mechanics to render them Lorentz invariant are therefore unjustified on physical grounds: there *are no* empirical findings which necessitate the alterations Einstein imposed. And as regards our use of Mach's Principle (or half of it, to be exact), it may not be without interest to note that Einstein him-self was profoundly inspired by this discovery: it is he, in fact, who coined its name. It strikes me as ironic, thus, that the very Principle which may have set him on the spoor of his "general" theory actu-ally validates what he seemed to abhor: geocentrism no less!

But lest there remain any doubt regarding the validity of taking geocentric reference frames to be stationary, let me refer to a recent paper—entitled *"Newton-Machian analysis of a Neo-tychonian model of planetary motions"*[12]—in which a physicist named Luka Popov calculates planetary orbits by means of Newtonian physics, based on a *geocentric* reference frame. In so doing, Popov has abro-gated, once and for all, the hegemony of heliocentrism, inaugurated in 1687 by Isaac Newton himself through the quasi-heliocentric[13] calculation of planetary orbits, based upon his newly-discovered "laws of motion" and infinitesimal calculus. Ever since that monu-mental breakthrough it has been an unquestioned dogma of West-ern science that "planet Earth" revolves around the Sun: once a year to be exact, with an orbital velocity on the order of 30 km/sec as we have been often enough reminded. But whereas the validity and indeed the accuracy of the Newtonian calculations have never been in doubt, Luka Popov appears to be the first physicist in history *to disprove* that they entail the aforesaid dogma: the notion, namely, that the Earth is a planet revolving around the Sun, or even permit us to infer that the Sun itself *is not* a planet revolving around the Earth. He rather confirms, by direct "Newton-Machian" calcula-tion, what classical physics, in conjunction with Mach's Principle, permits us to conclude: the fact, namely, that the "heliocentric" cos-mography can actually be obtained via Newtonian physics on a *geo-centric* basis.[14]

---

12. *Eur. J. Phys.* 34, 2 (2013): 383.

13. I say "quasi-heliocentric" because Newton placed the origin of his coordi-nate system, not at the center of the Sun, but at the center of gravity of the Sun-planet 2-body system.

14. The term "Neo-tychonian" need not detain us. Tycho Brahe, in the 16th cen-tury, conceived the remarkable idea that whereas the Sun rotates around the Earth, the remaining planets rotate around the Sun. This formulation embodies all the advantages of the Copernican theory, to which it is in fact isomorphic.

Let me repeat: *Luka Popov's result has broken the long-standing hegemony of heliocentrism.* It demonstrates, on the basis of Newtonian mechanics, that it is equally legitimate to claim that the Sun rotates (annually) around the Earth: it all depends on your choice of coordinates, *and geocentric coordinates are in fact legitimate.*

The picture changes drastically, however, the moment one takes electromagnetism into account: for now the Principle of Immobility comes into play, which, as we have seen, singles out the Earth from all other celestial bodies by the fact that it can be both stationary and central. What confronts us here constitutes evidently the very pinnacle of design: no wonder "relativists" of every stripe abhor the notion like the plague! So far from being a planet, the Earth can thus be viewed as the very antithesis: as the stationary center, namely, around which all other celestial bodies are constrained to revolve diurnally. And as to the authentic planets or "wanderers," beginning with the Sun: these do then execute, in addition, their appointed orbits around the Earth, very much as the ancient astronomers had ascertained.

Getting back to Albert Einstein: despite occasional references to "the Old One" (*"der Alte"*), he is evidently opposed to the notion that "a Divine Foot" could have a detectable effect upon the physical universe. He appears rather to accept the premise that "horizontal" causality by itself suffices to explain all that could possibly be of interest to the physicist, and moreover made it his task to discover the "ultimate" differential equations: the ones which supposedly account, with one hundred percent accuracy, for all that is measurable. He was irrevocably opposed, therefore, to the notion of quantum indeterminacy, convinced apparently that "beneath" the quantum level, horizontal causality reigns supreme. And based presumably upon these certainties, the great physicist pursued the one and only course left open: which is *to alter the classical equations of mechanics*—by fiat as it were—*to render them "relativistic."*

What I wish to emphasize is that Einsteinian relativity is actually predicated upon the assumption that *there can be no such thing as an immobile reference frame, a K_0 "at rest"*: it is this denial that leads quite naturally to at least the special theory of relativity. But given that there exists not a shred of empirical evidence in support of that denial, one sees that Einsteinian physics cannot but be based ultimately on ideological grounds. Yes, we *are* witnessing a "War Against Design": it is by no means a pious fiction! Modern science *is not*—and never *has been*—the "disinterested quest of truth" our textbook wisdom proclaims it to be. The example, to be sure, which most flagrantly contradicts that official narrative—to the point that any "unprogrammed" spectator can readily see it for himself—is doubtless the Darwinist theory of evolution, the hegemony of which remains intact, as we have seen, even after that hypothesis has been *mathematically* disproved.[15] The case of Einsteinian physics is of course far more difficult to "unmask"; and yet, the moment one brings "geocentrism" into the picture, the pieces fall quite readily into place. The first two paragraphs of Einstein's 1905 paper suffice already to raise the definitive questions: all one need do, when Einstein postulates his Principle of Relativity, is ask "*why?*": why alter the Newtonian equations? why suppose that they are in any way deficient? what experiment has told us so? Is it the Michelson-Morley? But in that case, why fault the classical equations of mechanics for the failure to detect a motion which *no previous experiment has ever verified*? Was the Michelson-Morley experiment not in fact designed precisely to verify that hypothesis? Is it sound scientific practice, then, to alter the fundamental equations of physics when they fail to accord with a preconceived conjecture?

The decisive fact is that the Einsteinian postulate is actually based not on scientific but on *philosophical* grounds. What stands at issue is not in truth a question of physics, but of philosophy: a *philosophy of physics* if you will. I see no need, moreover, to delineate that philosophical position, to spell out its principles and tenets. Suffice it to say that these evidently preclude the cosmos from being endowed with a structure which cannot, in principle, be accounted for in terms of *horizontal* causation alone. And that accounts for the

---

15. See footnote 3 above.

Einsteinian animus against geocentrism: for, like it or not, geocentrism calls for a *vertical* mode of causality.

The Empirical Argument Contra Einsteinian Physics

Given that the theoretical foundations of relativistic physics prove to be inherently ideological, it behooves us to consider the empirical side of the question: to examine how the Einsteinian theory fares when put to the test. And it will actually suffice to consider the special theory: for if this proves to be untenable, so does the general theory as well.

Let us recall in the first place that the special theory of relativity differs from classical physics only in the equations of mechanics, which it has altered by inserting the square root of $(1 - v^2/c^2)$ in certain locations, v being an observable velocity and c the speed of light. Now, given the enormous magnitude of c (approximately 300,000 km/sec) as compared to a normally observable velocity v, one sees that the factor in question will tend to be so close to 1 as to render its effect unmeasurable. If $v = 1000$ km/hr, for example, the square root of $(1 - v^2/c^2)$ will be $0.99999945\ldots$! The empirical verification of Einsteinian physics proves thus to be "challenging," to say the least.

It behooves us, first of all, to consider the fateful formula $E = mc^2$, which almost everyone in the world attributes to Albert Einstein's theory. Despite the fact, however, that Einstein did derive this formula from his special theory of relativity, it stems actually from its classical part: i.e., from the Maxwell equations for electromagnetic fields, which go back to 1865. The famous formula has consequently no bearing whatsoever on relativistic physics, a fact Einstein himself admitted in 1950.[16] Obviously, however, in the interim that fateful formula came to be viewed worldwide as the consummate

16. *Out of My Later Years* (New York: Philosophical Library, 1950), 282. For a brief history of the "atom bomb equation" I refer to Appendix 2 in the encyclopedic volume by Robert A. Sungenis and Robert J. Bennett, entitled *Galileo Was Wrong, the Church Was Right* (Catholic Apologetics International Publishing, 2008). Chapter 10 provides a concise and magisterial overview of the empirical literature bearing upon Einsteinian physics.

vindication of Einstein's theory: what indeed could be more convincing than the explosion of an atom bomb?

Misconceptions aside, the question whether special relativity has passed empirical muster proves to be an incurably technical issue. And no wonder, if at a speed of 1000 km/hr one needs to differentiate between 1 and 0.99999945! In his ground-breaking study,[17] Robert Bennett surveys more than three dozen experiments, covering a broad spectrum of empirical domains, which unfortunately hardly lend themselves to summary exposition comprehensible to non-specialists.

There are exceptions. For example, Einstein himself mentions the so-called Fizeau relation for the propagation of light in moving media as a confirmation of special relativity.[18] What stands at issue here is the speed of light in a moving liquid; and as might be expected, the subject proves indeed to be technical, involving such things as "the Fresnel drag coefficient" and the physics of Fizeau's "optical interferometer." But happily, one need not have the slightest idea what Fresnel and Fizeau were talking about! For it turns out that "Fizeau's relation"—which Einstein derived from special relativity and touted as a verification of his theory—can actually, once again, be obtained equally well from classical physics, a derivation which had in fact been carried out by the illustrious Henrick Lorentz himself.[19] As Bennet observes: "Unfortunately the denial of multiple causes for observed results is one of the key factors in current scientific rhetoric."

Leaving aside cases of this kind, what can one do to navigate a scientific literature which demands a high level of technical expertise in multiple fields? I propose to pursue a single trajectory based upon three interconnected experiments, which proves, I believe, to be definitive. It begins with the 1913 Sagnac experiment, in which an interferometer, mounted on a rotating platform, splits a beam of light, so that, with respect to the platform, one beam rotates clockwise and the other counterclockwise. As Bennett explains:

17. Ibid.
18. *The Meaning of Relativity*, 27.
19. *Galileo Was Wrong*, 446.

The time for the counter-rotating light to circle the ring is less than when stationary, so this beam is superluminal. The co-rotating beam takes a longer time to traverse the circle, so its speed is subluminal. In either case the speed of light exhibits anisotropy contrary to Special Relativity.[20]

The likely objection is that inasmuch as we are dealing with a "rotating" reference frame, special relativity does not apply. It happens, however, that Ruyong Wang *et al.* conducted an experiment in 2003, in which "the Sagnac effect is also obtained on a two-way linear path, by reversing a light beam sent out on a straight line on a moving platform and measuring the difference in return time."[21] What the Wang experiment indicates is that the speed of light is *not* in fact c in every inertial reference frame, as Einsteinian physics demands.

This leads to the question: are there other experiments which confirm this so-called Sagnac effect, or do the Sagnac-Wang experiments stand alone? Now it happens that the highly sophisticated Global Positioning System or GPS functions as a laboratory ideally suited to test the findings of Sagnac and Wang. For inasmuch as GPS operates by way of microwave beams connecting a terrestrial source to a satellite some 24,000 kilometers above the Earth, it is to be expected that "relativistic effects"—if such do exist—will come into play. What then does one find? "In 1984," Robert Bennett informs us, "GPS technician D.W. Allan and a team of international scientists measured the same effect on light as Sagnac did"! To be precise: "Alan and his colleagues found that microwave beams sent to an approaching GPS satellite take 50 nanoseconds less time to reach the satellite than beams sent to a receding satellite.... Once again, we have confirmation that the speed of light is not the same for all observers."[22] It happens, moreover, that this correction proves to be crucial to the correct functioning of the GPS: "Each GPS unit must, without exception, take into account the Sagnac

20. Ibid., 396.
21. Ibid., 403.
22. Ibid., 565.

effect," and the aforesaid 50-nanosecond difference is in fact "automatically built into the computer program for GPS."

However—unbelievable as it may sound—at this point a tale of deception begins to unfold: for not only is this contra-Einstein finding not acknowledged, it is artfully concealed. As Ruyong Wang and his associate Ronald Hatch testify: the Jet Propulsion Laboratory bases its calculations officially on a so-called "solar system barycentric frame"—*modified*, however, *so as to yield precisely the same results as an Earth-centered or so-called ECI reference frame!*[23] Now, in plain English, this is deceit. We have, at this point, drifted far from the textbook definition of science as "the unbiased quest of empirical truth"!

It remains to say at least a few words regarding a question obviously relevant to "the empirical status" of Einstein's theories: how, namely, does Einsteinian physics stand in relation to quantum theory? Let me note in the first place that quantum physics is in a way the very opposite of relativity theory: for so far from being "ideology driven," it imposed itself upon a generally reluctant scientific community; not therefore on ideological grounds, but evidently by force of necessity. Scientists accepted quantum physics for the simple reason that it proved to be the only theory capable of dealing with the newly-discovered "quantum phenomena." And from its inception the new physics functioned as the magic key which enabled physicists to unlock the secrets of the microworld, from the "algebra" of atomic spectra to the behavior of fundamental particles. And since quantum mechanics *à la* Heisenberg and Schrödinger merges into classical mechanics as we ascend into the macroworld—that is to say, let Planck's constant h tend to zero—the question presents itself whether there exists a modified or "corrected" quantum theory which similarly merges into *relativistic* mechanics.

Now let me note at the outset that I have never concerned myself

23. Ibid., 569.

seriously with that kind of physics: have not so much as read a paper dealing with any part of it. I speak thus as an outsider. There are two things, however, I can say with absolute certainty: first, that the effort to "marry" quantum theory with Einsteinian physics—which has been ongoing for a very long time, has enlisted a galaxy of brilliant physicists, and engendered some of the most dazzling examples of mathematical wizardry the world has ever seen—has failed abysmally to achieve its objective. And I vividly recall Michio Kaku, in a documentary film,[24] stretching his arms wide and raising his voice as he informs us that relativity and quantum theory differ ultimately *"by one hundred twenty orders of magnitude!"* I don't understand what exactly this means; but judging by the expression on Michio Kaku's face, it must be about as bad as such things can get.

But no one should actually be surprised. I ask myself: what has Einsteinian physics ever accomplished that one should search for a *relativistic* quantum theory in the first place? And in fact I regard it as yet another triumph of quantum physics that it has spurned the proffered union.

It should hardly come as a surprise that contemporary astrophysics—based as it is upon the general theory of relativity—has not fared too well. The grand expectations, fueled by the mystique of a "4-dimensional space-time" in which moving rods contract, clocks slow down, and the continuum itself curves in unimaginable ways, have not materialized: the facts of observation seem not to be onboard. From the outset unanticipated difficulties have cropped up which could be "explained away" only by invoking the virtually unlimited powers of the most abstruse mathematics. When for example, in the first second of the postulated "Big Bang," the expansion proves too slow, the resources of mathematical wizardry can provide us with something termed "inflation" to set the process back on course. Or when it turns out that there is not enough mat-

24. *The Principle.*

ter in the universe to produce gravitational fields strong enough for the formation of stars and galaxies, there are mathematical geniuses with a flair for particle physics who can make up the difference with something termed "dark matter." The requisite ingredient can in fact be supplied in numerous varieties and flavors: by the magic stroke of a pen there appear before us higgsinos, photinos, gluinos, quark nuggets, and many many more such marvels to meet our needs. Never mind that not one of these wonders has ever been detected: the fact that they are supportive of "Big Bang" theory is proof enough.

We need not multiply examples of this kind. What confronts us here is a strategy for keeping a scientific theory alive by means of *ad hoc* postulates, assumptions "picked out of thin air" for that very purpose. The technique had long served as a mainstay of Darwinist biology before it came to be employed in the service of Einsteinian cosmology. I find it an interesting question, pertaining to the philosophy of science, whether the end-product of such a process, assuming the sequence does converge, has yet even a scintilla of scientific validity: have we then, in other words, discovered a truth—or simply constructed a fantasy? We need not however resolve that issue in the case of Einsteinian cosmology: for by 1996, difficulties arising from empirical data came into view which no "*ad hoc* magic" could dispel.

The problem resides in an electromagnetic radiation field known as the CMB: let us pick up the story at this juncture. As Robert Bennett explains:

> The Cosmic Microwave Background is considered the most conclusive piece of evidence for the Big Bang by current cosmology. It is the isotropic radiation bath that permeates the entirety of the universe. Accidentally discovered in 1964, it was soon determined that the radiation was diffuse, emanated uniformly from all directions in the sky, and had a temperature of about 2.73 degrees Kelvin. It is now explained as a relic of the evolution of the universe.[25]

---

25. *Galileo Was Wrong*, 498.

The CMB is in fact regarded by theorists as a picture of the universe some 300,000 years after the Big Bang. Its isotropy, moreover, is tempered by "small" random fluctuations which in fact are needed to explain the formation of stars: it is for this reason that cheers went up, literally, when it was first announced that data from the COBE satellite had confirmed the existence of such statistical variations in the CMB.

What the cheering scientists did not know is that additional information regarding the CMB was in the offing, which would prove to be far less felicitous. For it happens that, not long thereafter, hints of an "axis" began to appear, spreading alarm within the astrophysics community: its initial designation as "the axis of evil" testifies to the fact that the phenomenon—if it were to prove real—is by no means propitious to the Big Bang. In hopes of putting these fears to rest, another satellite, named "Planck," outfitted with the most marvelous instruments—and lavishly protected against all conceivable "extraneous" radiation which might cause a non-existent axis to emerge—was put into orbit in 2009, at which point the scientists could do nothing more than wait and hope for the best. It was a "make-or-break" scenario; for if that "axis" were to prove real, no *ad hoc* hypothesis whatsoever could save the theory: it would in truth be the end of Big Bang cosmology. And the verdict did come in, and the dreaded axis was there, plain as day—as if drawn by the Finger of God.

Let us pause to understand why this discovery does in fact prove fatal to the Einsteinian cosmology. The fact is that Big Bang cosmology hinges upon the so-called Copernican Principle,[26] which stipulates that the cosmos is perfectly homogeneous when viewed on a sufficiently large scale. Besides exemplifying the Einsteinian denial of "design" to perfection, this Principle also proves indispensable to relativistic cosmology on technical grounds: for unless one postulates global symmetries which epitomize the very "design" Einsteinians are pledged to deny, it constitutes the one and only condition under which the pertinent field equations can actually be solved for the cosmos at large. The Einsteinians, therefore, had one chance,

---

26. Also termed the Cosmological Principle.

and one chance only, to arrive at a global cosmology; and when that axis, that fateful Line, appeared in the CMB, that prospect collapsed.

Yet there is more to the story: for it happens that the plane defined by that circular axis *coincides with the ecliptic of our solar system*; and for Einsteinians this constitutes indeed a worst-case scenario: for what was supposed to be an accidental "speck" within a galaxy—which itself is supposedly but an accidental speck in a universe bereft of order, bereft of design—this "accidental speck within an accidental speck" turns out to *define the global structure of the universe*! At the risk of sounding anthropomorphic, I surmise "the Old One" may have *smiled* when he traced that axis. Or perhaps—to venture yet another anthropomorphic surmise—may simply *have had enough*!

Unmasking "Anthropic Coincidence"

By the middle of the twentieth century, atomic physics and molecular biology had arrived at a point of vantage from which the existence of man upon "planet Earth" appeared so vastly improbable as to be, in effect, miraculous; and to folks who despise miracles, this poses a problem.

The central mystery resides in the fact that an exceedingly fine balance of the four fundamental forces known to physics is needed to render organic molecules stable enough to exist, which means that the basic constants of physics need be almost "infinitesimally" close to their given values—prompting the question: *why?* "What is a man," asks Carl Becker, "that the electron is mindful of him?"

What confronts us here in this "mindfulness" is evidently one of the most compelling and irrefutable instances of *design*. To the unprogrammed mind, moreover, this fact is immediately apparent: one recognizes the imprint of *design* through a quasi-direct realization that the phenomenon in question *could not*—by any stretch of the imagination—be the effect of *horizontal* or so-called "natural" causes. One doesn't require a university diploma or so much even as a high school education: the natural light of human intelligence suffices amply to arrive at that conclusion in a trice.

When it comes to the contemporary scientist, however, that normal power of comprehension seems no longer to be operative: for him the question "why the electron is mindful of man" constitutes a problem that calls ultimately for some kind of "hyper-physics" yet to be conceived. So he sets about to construct scenarios of the most imaginative kind to explain—or actually, explain away—this problematic "mindfulness," oblivious of the fact that he is leaving out of consideration what is actually the crucial point: namely, that *it takes*, not one, but *two modes of causality* to make a universe. These hyper-physicists are searching therefore—with indomitable determination no less—for something which in principle *cannot exist*. No wonder the search continues interminably to expand while it leads nowhere: one might as well scour the mathematical woods in search of a rational square root of 2! And no wonder, also, that the quest has fragmented into various technical domains defined by a *modus operandi* of their own, each fantastic in its own way. Meanwhile, as library shelves continue to bulge, the mystery of the electron's "mindfulness" remains as incomprehensible to the scientific *periti* as it had been when the search began more than half a century ago.

By the time John D. Barrow and Frank J. Tipler published their monumental survey,[27] this branch of "science" had burgeoned into a field almost rivalling the classical domains of physics. Having elsewhere presented an overview and analysis of this strange twentieth-century meta-physics,[28] I will restrict myself to what could perhaps be termed the mainline argument, leading step by wondrous step to that astonishing conception known as the "multiverse."

The first thing that presents itself to the contemporary mind when it comes to explaining origins is of course the idea of "evolution": the problem, in this instance, is to conceive how the physical universe as such—which supposedly forms the basis of everything—could itself "evolve." How could such a thing as the fine-structure constant, for example—a numerical constant of physics which happens to be 7.2973531×10^{-3}, failing which "we" would not exist—how could that constant have conceivably "evolved"? A brand-new conception, obviously, is called for at the very outset of

---

27. *The Anthropic Cosmological Principle* (Oxford University Press, 1986).
28. *Ancient Wisdom and Modern Misconceptions*, ch. 10.

such an inquiry. And here the ingenious idea presents itself that inasmuch as, *for us*, the universe is evidently not an unobserved entity, *this very fact* imposes certain conditions of a *physical* kind. And though, at first glance, that notion may appear to be tautologous—like saying "the universe is perceptible because it is perceived"—that seeming tautology proves actually to have teeth as a so-called "self-selection" principle.[29] It leads in fact to the first "anthropic principle" named WAP, the "W" standing for "weak." In the words of Barrow and Tipler, it affirms that "the observed values of all physical and cosmological quantities are not equally probable, but take on values restricted by the requirement that there exist sites where carbon-based life can evolve, and by the requirement that the Universe is old enough for it to have already done so."

We will pass over the fact that our hyper-physicists are apparently willing to base their conclusions upon the Darwinist hypothesis at a time when the discovery of the genome has already *de jure* invalidated that nineteenth-century conjecture. But let us continue: this WAP proved in any case to be less than sufficient, and was succeeded ere long by an SAP—"S" standing for "strong"—which asserts: "The universe must have those properties which allow life to develop within it at some stage of history." Yet that new so-called "principle"—which once again presupposes the Darwinist scenario and in truth explains nothing—that principle too does not yet suffice: for the question obviously remains from where and by what means one could obtain a universe satisfying that "strong" condition. And out of the maze of the purportedly "scientific" literature dealing with this issue, what might be termed a consensus appears to have emerged: following the lead of Stephen Hawking, a considerable portion of the scientific elite have opted for an infinite ensemble of possible universes, termed the "multiverse," as the ultimate solution to the riddle posed by the existence of our world.

There is a certain logic in this Ansatz; for in light of the SAP the

---

29. The idea was applied, for example, by Copernicus in the recognition that the phenomenon of retrograde motion in planets could be explained by the motion of the Earth-bound observer. In the context of the anthropic coincidence problematic, it was introduced by Brandon Carter in 1974.

question becomes: how then do we obtain a universe satisfying that stipulated condition? And there are, basically, only two options: by an act of creation of course, *or* by a "roll of the dice"—which evidently demands an adequate supply of "universes" from which an "SAP universe" can be drawn, as it were, "by chance."

Now, all this is of course perfectly insane, and brings home the lengths to which scientists of repute are willing to go in this ongoing "war against design." One cannot but ask oneself: whence comes this deep-rooted aversion—this profound animosity, one is tempted to say—*to the very conception of God?*

6

The Emergence
of the Tripartite Cosmos

With the discovery of quantum theory, the "Reign of Quantity" has entered its terminal phase. The shift from classical to quantum physics—which evidently is not compatible with the pre-quantum worldview—heralds the demise of that Reign: when the fundamental science stands in contradiction to the prevailing Weltanschauung, the latter is bound to give way.

Let us look at the matter more closely. Beginning with Galileo and Descartes, the "enlightened" portion of mankind succumbed to the surprisingly crude notion of a "clockwork" universe. Reformulated in the course of the nineteenth century in more abstract terms through the discovery of electromagnetism, it is in the schematic of Einsteinian physics that this mechanistic notion attained its most sophisticated form. Meanwhile, however, it came to pass with the advent of quantum theory that the idea of clockwork causality in whatever mode has been invalidated, once and for all, as the presiding paradigm: not even the dazzling mathematics of David Bohm—with its quasi-magical pilot wave—can controvert this fact, as we have seen.[1] The pre-quantum concept of a deterministic causality retains of course a certain validity in the classical limit—realized mathematically by letting Planck's constant h tend to zero—but fails irremediably on the plane of quantum theory.

But whereas the demise of determinism has been widely acknowledged, what has so far remained almost totally unrecog-

1. See p. 38 above.

nized is the fact that quantum physics demands[2] *two* supra-physical conceptions: one *etiological* and the other *ontological*. The first—what I term *vertical* causation—comes into view, as we have seen, in the act of measurement, and proves to be more basic and more powerful than the horizontal modes of causality known to the physicist; and the second, amazingly enough, is simply the affirmation of the actual world "in which we live, and move, and have our being": how strange that despite decades of almost desperate efforts to circumvent "quantum paradox," it has apparently never occurred to the quantum-reality theorists that such a world might actually exist!

These then are the twin recognitions which not only resolve the quantum enigma, but *de jure* terminate the Reign of Quantity. It matters little whether our scientific pundits recognize this fact or continue to espouse disqualified premises: like it or not, the cycle of history initiated by Copernicus and Galileo is now drawing to its close. When the foundational physics—which proves to be the most "astronomically" accurate science the world has ever seen—declares its own insufficiency and points beyond itself, the opinions of the reigning *periti* pale into insignificance: whether they elect to come aboard or not, history continues on its course.

How then does the resolution of "the quantum enigma" impact our worldview? In the first place it gives us back a "world" that *can be* viewed! One needs to recall that since the publication of Newton's *Principia* in 1687, the scientific pundits have imposed upon us a "world" that cannot be *viewed* at all. What has saved us from annihilation, meanwhile, is the fact that no one on Earth actually believes what the scientific *periti* advocate on that score: not even the top physicists themselves! To all except possibly the impaired, the sky is

2. It does so, not on the basis of quantum mechanics itself, but on the grounds of metaphysics—which is after all the reason why, to this day, "no one understands quantum theory."

still blue and roses red, except in those rare moments when one engages in scientistic speculations of a Cartesian kind: *then only* do we deny what otherwise we staunchly believe. Though well-nigh universally unobserved, the fact is that our scientistic Weltanschauung—to the extent that we have made it our own—has plunged us into a state of collective schizophrenia, an affliction scarcely compatible with sanity. The first effect, then, of the aforesaid resolution, is that it cures us at one stroke of this malaise, and renders it possible, in particular, to be a physicist while remaining perfectly sane.

My second point relates to Richard Feynman's remarkable dictum: "*No one understands quantum theory.*" It happens namely that the resolution of the quantum enigma enables us not only to "understand quantum theory," but to understand at the same time why previously "no one" *could.* The point is that the so-called quantum world cannot be comprehended without reference to the sense-perceptible or *corporeal:* the very realm the existence of which physicists have long been taught to deny. The reason, moreover, why the quantum world cannot be understood "on its own" is quite simply that *it does not in fact exist:* for as Heisenberg was the first to observe, that putative "world" consists of so-called particles which are not in truth "things," but *potentiae,* which do not "yet" exist.

But not only has it now become possible to "do physics" while remaining perfectly sane—and even to "understand" what one is doing—but now, by virtue of these recognitions, one can actually *do so better.* Thus we have come to understand not only what physics *can* do, but also what it can't: for it happens that the ontological interpretation of quantum theory has uncovered a hitherto unknown mode of causation more fundamental than the causality indigenous to the physical world. For as the resolution of the measurement problem has brought to light, *vertical causation trumps horizontal:* has power, namely, to abrogate or "re-initialize" the Schrödinger equation. And this is a game-changing discovery, for it tells us that quantum physics is not in truth the absolutely "fundamental" science one has taken it to be, but is in fact restricted in its scope to an "underworld" of mere *potentiae:* that so far from being a "theory of everything," there is rather point in saying that it is, in a sense, a theory "of nothing at all."

I will mention in passing that students of Oriental philosophy will not be altogether surprised: it has been known for a very long time by way of the *yin-yang* that existence cannot be reduced to a single principle: that "it takes two to exist." To put it in Aristotelian terms: it requires *hyle* plus *morphe* (the Latin *materia* and *forma*) to make a world. And herein resides the ontological heresy of modern physics, which has in effect sought to build a cosmos out of *hyle*— out of "matter"—alone.

The objection may be raised that physics has actually to do with *quantities*: that it constitutes after all "the science of measurement." True enough! But here again the Scholastics hold the key: "*Numerus stat ex parte materiae*"—"Number stems from the side of *materia*"—they declare. And this means that even if the physicist could know literally everything pertaining to the quantitative aspects of the cosmos, something absolutely basic and indeed "essential" would still elude his grasp.

Strange as it may sound to modern ears, what physics as such has left out of account is precisely the *active* principle of cosmic existence: the Aristotelian *morphe* corresponding to the *yang* side of the Chinese icon. And this "white spot in the black field" has now revealed itself on the quantum level in the form of *vertical causality*: it is something physics as we know it can neither comprehend nor ignore—because in fact that causality manifests the cosmogenetic Act itself.

All this was predictable from the start. The lapse into a fantasy-world began with the philosophy of René Descartes, upon which the current interpretation of our physics is based: by banishing the *qualities* from the real or "external" world, the French metaphysician has in effect cast out the *yang*-side of cosmic reality. We have said that "number" or *quantity* derives from the side of *materia*: it needs also however to be pointed out that the *qualitative* content of the world—what the Cartesians have downgraded to the status of mere "sensations"—stands on the side of *morphe*, of *form*. What is left, therefore, after the Cartesian intervention, is a kind of half-world which, in truth, as we have said, does not exist. Yet it is this semi-world, precisely, which Newtonian or "classical" physics has made its own, its "universe" over which that physics holds sway. What commends this scientistic claim, at least superficially, is the fact that physics is primarily concerned, not with what things *are*—or whether they even "exist"—but simply with *how they move*: its fundamental laws are *laws of motion* after all. What causes a thing to move, moreover, are generally other things, which act upon each other by way of a causal chain. One may think of it as a kind of domino-effect propagating through space, which constitutes what we have termed "*horizontal*" causality. It is actually surprising that this simple notion of causality has enabled the prodigies of prediction and control physics has wrought, persuading some of the brightest minds that it covers the entire ground; what on the other hand is not surprising in the least is that in fact it does not. Yet that recognition will take time to disseminate: physics at large has, after all, proclaimed for over four hundred years that the world is made up of Cartesian *res extensae* interacting in complex ways via *horizontal* chains of causality, and even the discovery of electromagnetism—"ethereal" though it be—did nothing to dislodge that inbred notion: the Newtonian "clockwork" paradigm may have been refined but was by no means abandoned.

The picture began to shift with the discovery of quantum physics, which disclosed the startling fact that *in the quantum world there are no res extensae at all*. Physics had finally descended, so to speak, to its own level, which proved to harbor *potentiae* in place of "actual" *things*. To put it in Scholastic terms: physics had now arrived at the level of *materia signata quantitate*, between *prima materia*—which properly speaking has no "existence" at all—and the lowest ontological stratum within the cosmic hierarchy, what I designate the *corporeal*. It is thus to this pseudo-world of *materia signata quantitate* beneath the corporeal that the objects of physics in truth belong, a fact which becomes apparent the moment physics has been divested of its metaphysical fantasies: has been "de-Cartesianized," one could say. The problem, however, is that whereas quantum physics itself has rejected the Cartesian presuppositions, the quantum physicists have not—which is precisely why the so-called "quantum reality problem" has proved for them to be *de facto* insoluble.

What presently concerns us is the fact that at the very moment when physics "descended," so to speak, to its own proper level, a *non-physical* mode of causation has come into view. We need to understand *why* it takes a "non-horizontal" causality to "manifest" the quantum world. Now it happens that the reason is not far to seek: for if the act of measurement does indeed entail a transition from the *physical* to the *corporeal* plane, then horizontal causality cannot take us there: for as previously noted, a transition between ontological planes can only be accomplished "instantaneously,"[3] and thus by way of *vertical* causation. The fact is that this hitherto unrecognized causality functions in this instance as the connecting link between the quantum world of *potentiae* and the *real* or *existent* world of corporeal entities. It actually makes perfect sense! Our connection with the quantum world hinges, after all, upon the act of measurement, which consequently requires a mode of causation *not* effected by causal chains. The moment, therefore, when physics attained to its rightful ontological status, VC was bound to enter the picture as the connecting link between the *quantum realm* and the *corporeal world*. From a metaphysical point of vantage, moreover, it can be seen that vertical causality is needed to supply the *yang* component of corporeal existence, which the quantum realm as such does not possess—in a word, that vertical causation is "form bestowing," and therefore inseparable from the cosmogenetic Act. One could in truth say that it pertains to the authentic "Big Bang" which acts—not "in time," some fifteen billion years ago—but in the very *nunc stans* in which "*God makes the universe and all things*," as Meister Eckhart declares.

Referring to post-Newtonian physics, Sir Arthur Eddington observed that "the concept of substance has disappeared." What has actually "disappeared," however, are the imagined *res extensae* which "classical" physics had spuriously presupposed. It is this ontological rectification, moreover, that has enabled physics to enter finally into its own proper domain, which proves to be cate-

---

3. See pp. 37–39 above.

gorically sub-corporeal—"sub-existential" in fact—for the simple reason that it is comprised exclusively of "quantitative" elements. What is missing in that so-called quantum world, as we have noted, is the *morphe* or *yang*-side of the coin: and that is precisely what vertical causality supplies or brings into play in the act of measurement, and in so doing, "actualizes" the quantum world "in part."

Getting back to knowing also what physics "can't do," I would like to emphasize how important this proves to be: think of the time and treasure wasted in the search for entities which prove to be *predictably* fictitious! Think of the "Big Bang" fiasco, not to speak of the Large Hadron Collider at CERN—which it took 100 nations to finance!—missioned to detect an array of "super-symmetry" particles conceived to exist in "space-time." My point is that a little *ontological* insight—sufficient, for example, to unmask the Einsteinian postulates—could suffice to forestall scenarios of that kind.

The deeper issue, however, is this: having discovered the existence of vertical causality, and attained some initial understanding regarding the manner of its action, can that "more-than-physical" knowledge be put to scientific use? Can it lead to discoveries of a *scientific* kind, and possibly to as yet undreamed-of applications? I regard this to be more likely than not.

&

The question presents itself, in particular, how the discovery of vertical causality impacts the biological sciences: for inasmuch as the distinction between animate and inanimate entities stems from their substantial form—from the fact, namely, that the substantial form of an animate creature is of a special kind, referred to traditionally as a *soul*—it follows that life and its phenomena constitute actually an effect of vertical causality. Our present biology, on the other hand, has eyes at best for the corporeal, which is to say that it views a living plant or animal as simply a "super-complicated" structure, which in the final count it conceived in *physical* terms. To the eyes of the contemporary biologist, it is thus ultimately the "tons" of specified information in the DNA that accounts for the observable phenomena: from the prevailing point of vantage there *is* after all nothing else that *could* enter the picture. Leaving aside the question how that "astronomical" complexity, embodied in that DNA, may have originated—which of course one is wont to answer in Darwinist terms—contemporary biology views a living organism thus as in effect a machine. It consequently perceives a plant or an animal as something which can in principle be understood "without residue" in terms of physics alone: that, when all is said and done, appears to be the underlying tenet upon which contemporary biology is based.[4]

The first point to be made is that this reduction of the animate to the inanimate—of the living to the merely "complex"—so far from being based upon scientific fact, is actually a groundless assumption, which gains strength from the fact that it is beyond our means to grasp whatever it may be that distinguishes the two. It amounts to saying that the living organism can only be what our methods of inquiry are in principle capable of detecting: that it must consequently reduce to a physical object, and that, at bottom, biology is no more than physics. But not only is this assertion unfounded, but as we have also come to recognize, it is in fact false: with the discovery of vertical causality the picture has radically changed. We now know not only that VC exists, but that it is in fact productive of corporeal being: not even a pebble can exist without a corresponding act of vertical causation. And this is a fact physics as such cannot grasp, let alone explain. The *a priori* notion, therefore, that physical science can account without residue for the phenomena of life— that living organisms reduce ultimately to a physical system—has thus been falsified: how can VC be left out of account in a living creature when it enters the picture even in a drop of water or a grain of sand?

The crucial question is whether the VC productive of a living creature can "override" the laws of physics, can in certain ways transgress these laws. To put it in Lagrangian terms: if we knew the morphology of a living organism perfectly at a given moment of

---

4. I do not wish to imply that such is the belief of *each and every* biologist; but though there may be exceptions, such appears to be indeed the rule.

time, could we then *in principle* calculate its behavior with perfect accuracy? Or taking "quantum effects" into account: can the behavior of a living entity "violate the laws of physics," be they classical or quantum-theoretic? What we are asking in effect is whether a living organism is actually *more* than a physical system; and according to the currently prevailing view—the prevailing *assumption*, to be precise—it is not. Yet in truth there is not, nor in fact *can there be* scientific evidence of any kind in support of that assumption. The very idea of regarding a living organism as a "physical system" proves to be incongruous, inasmuch as it leaves out of consideration the very essence of a living organism, which resides after all in its substantial form and manifests through acts of vertical causality. This soul-generated VC constitutes in fact the life-force or *élan vital* of the organism, which both "produces" its body or "corporeal sheath" and renders it *animate*.

I say this, of course, not on scientific but on metaphysical grounds, inasmuch as the very question proves in fact to be metaphysical. But so too does the aforesaid reductionism of the contemporary biologist! The claim that the phenomena of life can be understood, without residue, in purely physical terms, so far from constituting a scientific fact, proves thus to be but another scientistic myth: a misconception which, under the banner of "science," has befuddled not only the scientific *periti*, but Western civilization at large. What has rendered the public at large vulnerable in that regard is the vast store of bona-fide scientific knowledge concerning the morphology and physiology of living organisms contemporary biology has in fact brought to light. One forgets, however, that these discoveries do not begin to validate the reduction of the animate to the inanimate: one can arrive at the same bona-fide scientific knowledge *without* assuming that living organisms reduce to a molecular machine. For not only is this reductive tenet unprovable on scientific grounds, it turns out to be scientifically useless as well: so far from opening empirical doors, it does no more than shrink our field of vision.

What in fact differentiates the animate from the inanimate is the vertical causation emanating from a living organism's substantial form, which could however have no effect at all if it did not, in some ways, impact its physical dynamics: for so long as every constituent particle of the organism functions strictly according to the laws of physics—be they quantum theoretic or classical—there can *be* no such effect. The VC productive of an inanimate corporeal entity, on the other hand, does not thus impact or "override" physical causality; for as we have seen, it constitutes the active principle which imposes these very laws upon the given entity. The laws of classical physics, one might say, are in fact determined by the substantial forms definitive of corporeal entities. One must remember: "laws" derive from the side of *morphe* as opposed to *materia*. And if it be indeed the case that the vertical causality productive of the corporeal domain "actualizes" the laws of physics—as our interpretation of quantum theory implies—it is readily conceivable that the substantial forms definitive of the biosphere will in certain ways modify or override these "physical" laws. The phenomenology of living organisms suggests as much: for it proves indeed to be a salient characteristic of living creatures to counteract the dissipative and "equalizing" tendencies operative in the inanimate world.

Having suggested that the substantial forms productive of the biosphere (what is normally termed a "soul") may be capable of "overriding" the laws of physics, it is time to recall that *in fact they do*. For as we have had occasion to see in the case of a human being, there are indeed scientific grounds in support of the tenet that man is endowed with what is traditionally termed "free will," which entails that he is capable of actions based upon *vertical* causation. The fundamental axiom of contemporary biology—the supposition, namely, that a living organism reduces to a physical entity—has thereby been disproved.

The fact is that our present-day biology is restricted in its scope to the physical substrate of a living organism: its "outermost shell" or cadaver one can say. Meanwhile these biological sciences continue to advance by leaps and bounds—without however coming one step closer to understanding what it is that differentiates a living creature from an inanimate entity: what, in other words, "enlivens" or animates a plant or an animal. At bottom we know neither what life is nor how it functions: we are acquainted only with its morphological and physiological feats. And this entails, let me add parenthetically, that the door to the paranormal and indeed the "miraculous" has not been closed.

∾

A few more words regarding the vexed question of "free will" may therefore be in order: for inasmuch as the behavior of living creatures is not fully determined by the laws of physics, it can be said that even an amoeba possesses that attribute in some degree. The tiniest living organism, thus, is more than an automaton, incomparably more than a mechanism driven by forces satisfying the equations of physics, as we have been taught to believe. Such forces "obeying the laws of physics" do of course enter the picture—but only in a peripheral capacity: they apply so to speak to "the outer shell," the cadaver as we have said. One catches a glimpse of this fact when one observes a living creature at the moment of death, when the soul separates from the body: whereas all the marvelous morphology is still in place, that body no longer functions as a living organism.

Getting back to "freedom of the will," it is to be noted that this capacity is something worlds removed from the "non-automatic" behavior of an animal: for that kind of "freedom" applies—not to amoebae or insects—but to man alone. And this brings to light another fundamental fact our biology fails to discern: there is a profound *ontological* distinction, namely, between the soul or *anima* of an animal and that of a human being. What renders us human is not simply a "soul," but what is termed a *rational* soul, which is something more, something incomparably greater. And this fact alone, let us note, not only falsifies Darwinism of any stripe, but brings to light its venom: for in thus depriving man of what is in truth "the image of God"—what Meister Eckhart refers to even as a *Vünkelin* or "little spark" of the Logos, of God Himself as it were—these modern-day biologists reduce him to the status of an animal.

The point to be grasped is that the biosphere is not to be conceived as an unbroken continuity, which is to say that there exist gaps between species and genera which no amount of horizontal causation can bridge. The fact is that the so-called "tree of life" exhibits an architecture, a hierarchic structure, with the *anthropos* at its very peak. Like the cosmos at large—with the Earth at its center—the biosphere exemplifies *design,* which is something a science based exclusively on horizontal causality simply cannot comprehend. I would note, therefore, that under these auspices Darwinism is *de facto* unavoidable, which explains why the scientific community refuses to acknowledge the fact that it proves to be scientifically untenable. As Ernest Mayr said in reference to calculations establishing the astronomical improbability of evolutionary origin in the case of an eye: "We are comforted by the fact that evolution has occurred."[5]

What impedes contemporary biology categorically and drastically restricts its purview stems from its failure to recognize the existence, necessity, and function of vertical causation; and inasmuch as the animate stands above the inorganic, that deficiency proves to be all the more debilitating. The great challenge, now, is to rectify these deficiencies; and whereas the prospect is doubtless challenging in the extreme, it can hardly be declared impossible.

---

5. Phillip Johnson, *Darwin on Trial* (Downers Grove, Il: Intervarsity Press, 1993), 38.

7

The Primacy
of Vertical Causality

Vertical causality was identified in the context of quantum measurement: as the mode of causation, namely, which effects the transition from the physical to the corporeal domain. There exist other physical facts, moreover, that prove to be likewise indicative of VC: quantum entanglement, for instance, and the associated phenomenon of non-locality. When the measurement of an attribute of a particle at a point A *instantly* affects the state of its twin particle at B—conceivably light-years distant from A—the causality at issue *cannot* but be vertical. What gives rise to quantum entanglement, moreover, are interactions between the wave function and a *corporeal* entity, a fact which, once again, confirms that *vertical causality acts upon a quantum system by way of the corporeal plane*: that it "descends," so to speak, from the corporeal to the physical.

It behooves us now to "step back" and look at the etiological picture from a strictly ontological point of view. As stated at the outset, based upon what some have termed *cosmologia perennis*, the integral cosmos proves to be *ontologically tripartite*, and can be represented iconically by a circle, in which the circumference stands for the *corporeal* world, the center for the *spiritual*, and the interior for the *intermediary*.[1] It needs moreover to be clearly understood that these three components of the iconic circle correspond in truth to

---

1. It is vital to note that these three basic components of the cosmos have their counterparts in the *anthropos*, the human microcosm, which divides analogously into *corpus, anima,* and *spiritus.*

ontological domains of the integral cosmos which can be specified in terms of two *bounds*: the corporeal by space and time, the *subtle* or *intermediary*[2] by time alone, and the *spiritual* or *celestial* by the fact that it is subject to neither bound. What in the iconic representation appears thus to be the least of the domains—inasmuch as it has neither spatial extension nor temporal duration—proves thus to be actually the greatest: the ontological domain which in truth encompasses both the corporeal and the intermediary realms.[3]

It is worthy of note, moreover, how drastically even our truncated cosmos, as conceived in contemporary cosmology, has actually *shrunk*; and one might add that the concomitant explosion in both its temporal and spatial extension—as measured supposedly in billions of years and light-years—merely exacerbates its indigence. Despite the official bluster, the fact remains that, compared to the integral cosmos contemplated perennially by the wise, that "brave new universe" amounts to little more than a speck of dust. Supposedly measuring billions of light-years, it is in truth too indigent to be envisioned at all: to do so one needs first to embellish that postulated universe with attributes it is actually unable to possess.

A philosophically cogent cosmology cannot but be based on the recognition that the cosmos originated in a cosmogenetic Act which perforce is supratemporal, for the simple reason that time pertains to the cosmos alone: "*The world was created, not **in** time, but **with***

---

2. This is what has been termed the "astral plane" in occultist circles, and what in Orthodox Christianity is referred to as the "aerial world."

3. One should not fail to observe that this connects profoundly with various Christic sayings, beginning perhaps with the logion: "*Behold, the kingdom of heaven is within you*" (Luke 17:21). It may be of interest to note, moreover, that, according to the *Mandukya Upanishad*, the triadic constitution of the *anthropos* corresponds (in ascending order) to the waking state, the dream state, and the state of deep sleep, in which we mortals are normally not conscious at all; as one reads in the *Bhagavad Gita*: "In that which is night to all beings, the in-gathered man is awake; and where all beings are awake, that is night to the renunciate who *sees*."

time," St. Augustine observes. "Prior" to this inscrutable Act, nothing whatsoever existed—except of course the Universal Cause of all. Yet, surprisingly perhaps, this way of looking at cosmogenesis is yet somewhat incomplete: for according to the Aristotelian-Thomistic ontology—its so-called hylomorphism—something does in a way "pre-exist" the effect of the cosmogenetic Act: i.e., a certain "receptivity" or "recipient," if you will, termed *hyle* or *prima materia*, which is receptive of *morphe* or *form*, and in conjunction with *morphe* gives rise to the actual universe.[4] And that primary *morphe*, united thus to *materia*, gives rise to *substantial form*, which is what bestows reality upon a cosmic entity, what both causes it to *exist* and enables it to *act*: i.e., to deploy a *vertical* causality of its own.

This brings us finally to the fundamental questions: whence then does *horizontal* causation arise, and what constitutes its field of action? Now the answer to the first is virtually self-evident: *What gives rise to **horizontal** causality can be none other than **vertical** causation.* And as to its field of action, this too is not hard to discern: *The sphere of action of a horizontal cause can be none other than the **corporeal** domain*, for the simple reason that horizontal causation entails a transmission through space, and it happens that the corporeal world constitutes the one and only *spatio-temporal* domain; we must bear in mind that the spatial bound ceases to apply "above" the corporeal plane.

It needs however to be noted that horizontal causality does also in a sense act "below" the corporeal plane, that is to say, on the quantum level,[5] where it applies to entities "midway between being and non-being."[6] For whereas these entities may indeed be "less than real," the associated horizontal causality—as represented, say, by the Schrödinger equation—proves to be the most mathematically accurate physics mankind has ever known. What confronts us here is a "real" causality governing "less than real" entities.

Having shown that horizontal causation—whether acting on the

---

4. This corresponds evidently to what *Genesis* terms "the waters" in 1:2.

5. As I have argued elsewhere, the corporeal and the physical domains share one and the same space-time. See *The Quantum Enigma*, 40.

6. In Heisenberg's famous words.

corporeal or on the physical plane—constitutes an effect of vertical causes, it remains now to consider whether the latter are perforce cosmogenetic, or whether VC arising from a substantial form can be likewise productive of horizontal causality. To this end we need to take into account an obvious distinction: it is one thing to give rise to horizontal causality "*ex nihilo*," as it were—and quite another to *affect* or impact an existing causal chain (for example, by "re-initializing" the wave-equation). It thus becomes apparent that whereas it must be the cosmogenetic Act itself that actually gives rise to horizontal causation, secondary VC has nonetheless power to act upon existing chains of horizontal causality, to affect and alter them as we have had occasion to note: the vertical causality emanating from the substantial form of a pebble, for instance, has power to impede its multilocation. And let us not fail to recall at this juncture what we have said in the preceding chapter in reference to biology: that when it comes to substantial forms definitive of the animate order—the kind termed an "*anima*"—this capacity to "override" what we term the laws of physics is in fact definitive of the biosphere.

Getting back to the so-called quantum world, let us remind ourselves that it constitutes a *materia signata quantitate*: a realm midway between *prima materia* or "pure receptivity" and corporeal being, endowed with purely *quantitative* attributes. What is it, then, that could have effected its formation: by what process of causality was quantity "added" as it were to *prima materia*? This is still something of a mystery. Here the *cosmologia perennis*, which has served as our guiding light up to this point, is of little help, inasmuch as nothing remotely resembling the quantum realm was ever conceived in pre-modern times. The crucial question is whether John Wheeler was right when he claimed that physics deals ultimately with a "participatory universe": that in some way this *materia signata quantitate* is actually "constructed" by the *modus operandi* of the physicist. There appear moreover to be fairly cogent grounds to conclude that such may indeed be the case: it happens that the pioneering work of

Sir Arthur Eddington, which entails as much, has been strikingly confirmed in recent times by a physicist named Roy Frieden, who should by right be far better known than he is.[7] I would point out, moreover, that the notion of a "participatory universe"—the idea that the physical universe is in a sense "constructed"—is strongly supported by the recognition that corporeal entities can indeed "act" upon the subcorporeal realm by way of vertical causation. And I will add parenthetically that an inquiry into that hypothetical "construction of the physical universe" *in light of vertical causality* strikes me as the ideal—and perhaps even as the only viable—starting point to arrive at a deepened understanding of physics: an understanding, namely, which brings to light the function of vertical causality, its intrinsic connection with horizontal causation. Yet be that as it may, on metaphysical grounds the fundamental fact remains that the quantum realm—like every other ontological domain—constitutes in the final count an effect of vertical causation.

What then is the *raison d'être* of *horizontal* causality: what constitutes its cosmic "function," so to speak? Now the salient characteristic of horizontal causation is that it has to do exclusively with *quantities*: with the *quantitative* side of cosmic existence. Not with quantity *per se* however, but with a certain kind of quantity: the kind, namely, which is inherently *spatial* and hence indigenous to the corporeal domain. And that, I surmise, is the kind referred to as "*numerus*" in the Scholastic dictum "*numerus stat ex parte materiae*" ("number derives from the side of *materia*"): the kind, namely, which measures or "metes out" spatial extension. And let us note that this is the very bound which defines the corporeal domain: one might refer to it as "extensive" quantity—the kind expressed by real numbers—as distinguished from quantity defined by integers and their ratios, which unlike the former has a significance by no means restricted to the corporeal domain.[8] Moreover, inasmuch as *time* (in

7. On this question I refer to *Ancient Wisdom and Modern Misconceptions*, ch. 2.
8. That is the reason why music, for example, with its harmonic and rhythmic ratios, can literally "lift us out of this world." The quantities in question here—significantly termed "rational"—are in a sense "qualitative," and pertain to a branch of

the sense of duration) is likewise measured by way of spatial extension, it too can be expressed in terms of real numbers.

Which brings us to the crucial point: *horizontal causality, as known to physics, assumes the form of a differential equation relating spatial and temporal magnitudes, and reduces thus to a "law of motion."* It needs however to be recognized that this law itself is imposed by an act of *vertical* causation: to claim otherwise is to put the cart before the horse. Given that the corporeal world originates in an ontological domain where there *is no* spatial extension at all— and where consequently the equations of physics do not apply—it follows that the spatial and temporal bounds, which these equations presuppose, cannot themselves be the result of horizontal causes. It can thus be affirmed as a theorem of authentic cosmology that *the fundamental laws of physics—expressive of horizontal causality—are based on vertical causation.*

We see from these cursory reflections that the scope and efficacy of horizontal causality within the integral cosmos turns out to be quite limited: not only is horizontal causality subsidiary to vertical, but its sphere of action is restricted to the corporeal and subcorporeal domains, what might symbolically be termed "the lower third" of the integral cosmos. To which one should add that as one ascends the *scala naturae* within the corporeal domain itself, the efficacy of horizontal causality is progressively diminished through the incursion of vertical modes. In terms of the traditional "mineral, plant, animal, and anthropic" partition, it appears that the hegemony of horizontal causation is restricted at best to the "mineral" or inorganic domain.

To explore the implications of this fundamental etiological fact for the sciences, for philosophy, and above all, for an understanding of man, of his origin and destiny—this is a task we leave for others to take up.

---

mathematical science that may be characterized as *"harmonic,"* which moreover played a decisive role in antiquity in support of the arts, the sciences, and even the spiritual life. All but forgotten in modern times, I surmise it will be rediscovered after the *"reign of numerus"* comes to an end. It richly deserves to be: for even as qualities trump mere quantity, so does the science of "harmonic" numbers outrank our contemporary mathematics in the larger scheme of things.

Postscript

This brings to a close our brief reflections on the scientific significance and implications of vertical causality. It remains to point out that having thus initiated what might broadly be termed *a rediscovery of the vertical dimension*, we may have prepared the ground for a shift in the Weltanschauung of Western civilization. I believe, moreover, that a scientific *metanoia*, based on a rediscovery of vertical causation, is apt to inaugurate a cultural *metanoia* as well, which may "open doors" bolted shut centuries ago.[1] Above all, it may enable men and women to discern, once again, the *raison d'être* of human birth, which is and ever shall be *the attainment of life eternal in union with God*. We have been collectively distracted and deviated for centuries from catching so much as a glimpse of that God-given imperative: has the time perhaps arrived when that descending arc of history will come to an end? Such appears indeed to be the case.

That arc began in a very real sense with Galileo's hypothesized displacement of the Earth. It needs however to be understood that this conjecture does not stand alone: for it happens that the decentralization of the Earth goes hand in hand with a corresponding decentralization of man. What has in effect been lost are both the macro- and microcosmic manifestation of that central point in the cosmic icon: that *"pivot around which the primordial wheel revolves."* There are in truth *two* centers: the macrocosmic and its counterpart in the microcosm, the *anthropos*; and the two centers are in fact inseparable. How, then, are they connected? And by now the answer cannot but stare us in the face: *that universal and transcendent Cen-*

---

1. On the relation between "science" and culture I refer to *Ancient Wisdom and Modern Misconceptions*, especially the chapter entitled "Science and the Restoration of Culture."

ter of the cosmos is connected to its counterpart in man[2] by an act of vertical causality, which is none other than the cosmogenetic Act itself. Neither spatial distance nor temporal duration, thus, separates *our* Center from that *"pivot"* around which *"the primordial wheel revolves."* And this, I surmise, constitutes the Mystery wise men have pondered ever since the world began: their Quest has ever been for that *"punto dello stelo"* hidden deep within the heart, which is *"the eye of the needle"* through which *"the rich man"* cannot pass, and the *"narrow gate"* the *"pure in heart"* alone can enter.

How then did the Galilean intervention impact this Quest, this *longing*, however dimmed? It did so, ontologically, through the sub-jectivation of the qualities, and cosmographically, by the denial of geocentric cosmology. What remains, following these twin reduc-tions, is on the one hand the phantasm of a clockwork universe driven by a horizontal causality, and on the other a de-centered humanity: for when the cosmos loses its center, so does the micro-cosm, so as a rule does man. The overall impact of the Galilean intervention proves thus to be twofold: on the one hand what René Guénon refers to as *"the reign of quantity"* engendered by Cartesian bifurcation, and on the other what might well be termed *"the reign of relativity"* symptomatic of a decentralized humanity in a decentral-ized universe. The congruity of God, man, and cosmos became thus newly compromised, and in consequence of this breach the *anthro-pos* himself has begun to disintegrate at an unprecedented rate: *the Galilean impact upon humanity could thus be viewed as a second Fall.*[3]

In light of these reflections it is evident that the impact of the Galilean revolution upon Christianity and Christian culture at large was in fact bound to be fatal. *Christian civilization has need of the pre-Galilean worldview*—and this fact was recognized from the start by those who had "eyes to see": think of the impassioned words of John Donne, penned in the year 1611, when the Galilean revolution had barely begun: *"And new philosophy calls all in doubt,"* he laments; *"'Tis all in pieces, all coherence gone,"* he cries! Yet no one has made the point more sharply than Herman Wouk when he proclaimed

---

2. Which can be identified with his substantial form or soul.
3. On this issue I refer to "Progress in Retrospect" in *Cosmos and Transcendence.*

that Christianity has been *dying* "ever since Galileo cut its throat." I find it tragic that our contemporary theologians and churchmen seem, almost without exception, to have not so much as the faintest idea what Herman Wouk was talking about—which only goes to show, however, how profoundly right he was.

And this brings us finally to the crucial point: *in light of the facts delineated in this monograph, it appears that the Galilean arc of history is presently drawing to its close:* the rediscovery of vertical causation alone—along with the resultant unmasking of Einsteinian relativity—implies as much. For as we have come to see, the recognition of vertical causation opens the door to a rediscovery of the integral cosmos—the actual world in which we *"live, and move, and have our being"*—which not only exonerates geocentrism, but brings to light the existence and the ubiquity of the veritable Center.

Let Christians—and all who bow before God—rejoice: the scourge of relativism and irreligion has now been dealt a mortal blow! Following four centuries of intellectual chaos and *de facto* incarceration within his own distraught psyche, *homo religiosus* is now at liberty, once again, to step out into the God-given world, which proves to be—not a mechanism, nor some spooky quantum realm—but its very opposite: a *theophany* ultimately, in which *"the invisible things of Him from the creation of the world are clearly seen, being understood by the things that are made, even His eternal power and Godhead."*[4]

---

4. Rom. 1:20.

PART II

Is Science
Through With God?

A Philosophical Essay

Jean Borella

Translated by
G. John Champoux

Preface

I n a recent book, the famous physicist Stephen Hawking says that advances in science now prove the futility of the "God" hypothesis. Is this true? And to begin with, what does that even mean? Are the beliefs Stephen Hawking thrusts upon us, and especially the idea of God he and the atheists put forward, philosophically serious? This is the question we would like to examine in this brief essay. Not to establish, contrary to Hawking—which would require lengthy explanations—that science proves God, even though this seems obvious to us, but to ask: What is atheism's idea of "theism"? We will quite rightly see, then, that the atheist discourse, as such, quite simply does not know "what" it is talking about.

1

How Science
Became Atheistic

"My religion," declares Einstein, "consists of a humble admiration of the illimitable superior spirit who reveals himself in the slight details we are able to perceive with our frail and feeble minds. That deeply emotional conviction of the presence of a superior reasoning power, which is revealed in the incomprehensible universe, forms my idea of God."[1] Surely the adjective "emotional" can weaken the scope of this statement by giving it the sense of a merely subjective opinion. Yet its meaning is clear; and, coming from one of the greatest scientific geniuses of modern times, it should command the attention of our contemporaries. But this is not at all the case.

For more than three centuries our civilization has been convinced that science[2] has proven atheism—a proof all the more assured since this science is deemed to sustain the only reliable discourse on the nature of beings and things, on the structure and forces of the universe. The weight of this conviction has disqualified all other discourse. In particular, religious discourse has been radically devalued when it has claimed to pronounce on points of cosmogony (the formation of the world) or cosmology (the general organization of the universe and functioning of its component parts). Many believers, whether the simple faithful or learned exe-

---

1. Lincoln Barnett, *The Universe and Dr. Einstein* (New York: Dover Publications, 1948), 109.
2. It is a "science" very poorly known save by means of what the mass media tells us about it.

getes and theologians, have been persuaded that religious discourse must refrain from any proposal that might encroach upon the domain of science, and confine itself to the domains of spirituality (the relationship of the soul with God) or social morality (the relationship of man with his fellow men). And as regards the cosmogonic or cosmological declarations of sacred scripture, only *mythological residues* ought to be seen there, which in no way affect God's authority, and which must be interpreted, at best, as symbols with, moreover, quite simple meanings—for all these accounts say only one thing: "God has done everything and governs everything"; to be concerned about how the details of their literal sense relate to physical reality is only a waste of time.

The same goes for metaphysical discourse. Less naive, less mythological, and much more rational than that of religion, it is nonetheless still stricken with the same vanity as religious discourse insofar as it believes it can go beyond, or even ignore, the data of experimental science and claim access to the basic principles of reality. True, this claim was relatively admissible when science was in its infancy, thus offering philosophy's speculations ample space for uncertainty wherever given free rein. But this is no longer the case today, although we are not always aware of it.

This is precisely the subject of Stephen Hawking's recent book *The Grand Design*: not to demonstrate—which is all too obvious—the nonexistence of God, but, more radically, to explain why science does not really need this (religious or philosophical) idea of God to account in a completely satisfactory way for the existence and order of the world—a thesis that is certainly not new, but appears all the more convincing because expounded by one of the most famous scientists of our time, who, because of the terrible infirmity with which he was afflicted (oral expression precluded, able to communicate only with the help of a few hand movements) has been invested with the aura of a true scientific hero. It is not only a question, for Hawking, of repeating what was already said a few centuries ago, but of showing that the moment has now come, in all objectivity, when science is really able to provide an exhaustive explanation of the universe (which was not the case in previous centuries), and that such conclusions must be drawn.

Our intention is not to scientifically refute Hawking's book,[3] which we mention only for its exemplary significance. Besides the fact that such a refutation would far exceed our competence, it is important to note that this book has been the subject of a particularly well-grounded critique by a recognized scientist, Wolfgang Smith, a leading mathematician and renowned physicist who has taught at some of the most prestigious universities in the United States and who, in particular, helped to mathematically solve the problem of the space shuttle's reentry into the atmosphere. In addition, this high-ranking scientist is someone with a speculative turn of mind, who has never given up "thinking" the scientific process and has learned from the most important philosophers of both East and West. The book he devoted to this refutation[4] is titled *Science and Myth*. And what Wolfgang Smith denounces in this text is not only the "fictional" character of Stephen Hawking's *physical* findings, but also his ignorance of philosophical rationality and his misunderstanding of major metaphysical insights. For these latter alone allow access to an *intelligible* conception of the *reality* made known to us by the discoveries of contemporary science. It is essentially the theory of *quanta* which, as Wolfgang Smith points out, is the only theory, without exception (including that of general relativity), that no fact has so far contradicted.

The work of refutation having been done (and done well), what remains is for the philosopher to show how common Western thinking—of which Stephen Hawking's book is a singularly vigorous manifestation—has come to its resolute atheism and complete rejection of all metaphysics. As for "what remains," it suffices to say that we cannot tell the full story in the next few pages. We must content ourselves with mentioning some major stages of this his-

3. Stephen Hawking and Leonard Mlodinow, *The Grand Design*. In a recent interview with João Medeiros (*Wired Magazine*, December 2017), Hawking states that human intelligence could be replaced soon by a much more powerful artificial intelligence, which betrays a very "artificial" idea of intelligence. The intelligence is not essentially a faculty for combining data, but for grasping a meaning. Moreover, the mere combination of data actually presupposes non-material connections.

4. *Science and Myth: With a Response to Stephen Hawking's* The Grand Design (Tacoma, WA: Angelico Press/Sophia Perennis, 2012).

tory, our overriding concern being not only to report some well-known facts (which is history in the strict sense) but also, and mainly, to stress their epistemological significance—which is a matter of philosophy. Hence the subtitle of our study: "Philosophical Essay." Essentially, this involves critically examining the cosmogonic and cosmological conclusions that Hawking's book argues and illustrates, to show to what degree of metaphysical lack of understanding "scientific" modernism has come today.

2

Scientific Physics and Philosophical Fiction

We have emphasized above the title of Wolfgang Smith's book: *Science and Myth*. The term "myth" might seem surprising. Is it not rather philosophy, and even more religion, that is mythical or fictional, that is, a discourse that invents the real according to its own imagination? How can we bring such an accusation, not against science in general, but against a certain scientific discourse?

And first, is this really a reproach? Is not the scientific process obliged to claim, paradoxically, a certain right to (well-founded) fiction? Let us go further. An aspect of fiction is unavoidable when dealing with considerations of a cosmological and cosmogonic nature—that is, considerations undertaken not solely to observe and register (the first step of science) the data provided by a methodically experienced reality, or to translate it into mathematical language, but to think about this data in itself, according to the requirements of reality's overall intelligibility, and so to "conceptually imagine" the data's formation and the causality of its functioning. We are no longer quite in the field of science (from a strictly positivist point of view), but we are obviously entering into that of philosophy, which, being unable to claim the same degree of objectivity and truth as science, in a way, would be allowed to engage in conjectures and so in "fictions."

However, we must agree on the meaning we give to "fiction." If this is an invention unconcerned with reality or rationality, nothing can justify its use in philosophy, as if philosophy is doomed by nature to this fiction while—even though philosophy is inevitably part and parcel of science—science is excused from assenting to it. In truth, and for those who have objectively studied the great philosophers, it is clear that, given such a conception of fiction, philosophy is not entitled to rely on it. Contrary to the opinion which sees in philosophy only gratuitous hypotheses and unfounded claims, it must be said that philosophy, as much as science, seeks to arrive at an exact knowledge of what is. In this, there is no difference between the two, and if there is a really philosophical aspect of science insofar as it is not content with a mathematical description of reality, there is also a truly scientific aspect of philosophy in that it does not content itself with simply reshuffling presumptions. Both disciplines, that is, seek to *think* about reality in its truth. It would be good to reread what Bergson and Ruyer have written about this.[1]

But if we give "fiction," as is only right, a *positive* meaning—the one we have in mind when we speak of conceptual imagination—we also have the right to justify its use in science. A famous example will aid in understanding what is meant here: in his great work on *The Mathematical Principles of Natural Philosophy* (in the 1713 "General Scholium"), Newton asserts, with reference to the fact of universal gravitation, the "*non fingo*"—literally, "I-do-not-feign"—hypothesis. "Feign" here means not to deceive or to believe what is not, but to come up with a rational hypothesis to account for gravitational attraction[2] (an attraction that remains unexplained to this day). "Feign" is derived from the Latin *fingo*, which gives us *fictus* in Latin and, in English, *fictitious* and *fiction*; it can therefore mean "imagine," but in the neutral sense of shaping with one's mind, forming a hypothesis, or a well-founded supposition. When such an act of

---

1. Cf. Henri Bergson, *Duration and Simultaneity*, trans. L. Jacobson (Indianapolis, New York, Kansas City: Bobbs-Merrill, 1965), 5, 9–10; Raymond Ruyer, "La philosophie unie à la science," *Encyclopédie Française*, ed. Anatole de Monzie, vol. 19 (Paris: Larousse, 1957), 6–10. As for Stephen Hawking, he declares without further ado: "Philosophy is dead [because] it has not kept up with modern developments in science" (5), which, after a reading of Bergson and Ruyer, appears unbelievable.

2. Let us recall that we must not identify the attraction of gravity with the weight of a body. Attraction is exerted on a body's center of gravity. Thus all bodies fall at the same speed in a vacuum: a locomotive and a grain of sand arrive at the same time at the end of their fall in a void.

imagining is not possible and whenever someone persists in seeking to invent "reasons" contrary to all reason and all that one knows of the real, then, rather than "fictitious" we might speak of "fictional."

Be that as it may, human thinking has no more right to the fictional in philosophy than it has in science, which implies in particular that one's thinking must retain the same rigorous attention when it speaks of philosophy, even someone else's philosophy, as well as when it analyzes the work of scholars outside of one's own field. There should be no contempt or casual disregard for the great metaphysical texts. Now—and this is where Hawking's approach goes from science to the fictional—the illustrious physicist treats the greatest questions of philosophy with an almost complete ignorance of what major philosophers have said and of their argued *reasons* for establishing their theses.[3] No more than in science can one say just anything in philosophy. It may be objected that science has so radically altered all our ideas about time, space, matter, life, reality, the world, etc., that it no longer speaks of the same things as those philosophers. Is this possible? As new as all these notions are now, they nevertheless retain the identity of their designations, which cannot be just in name only. Hawking's enterprise proves this, moreover, since his intent is to bring different answers to these very questions of philosophy. And so, to be able to do this intelligently, the answers of the philosophers, at least of the most influential, should be known and meditated on. Such is not the case.

---

3. His work, it is true, begins with a historical reminder of the stages of science in ancient Greece. The facts mentioned are generally correct, but the philosophical interpretations offered are often quite approximate, if not false. Thus, to wonder whether, according to Aristotle, God had any latitude in choosing the laws of nature (cf. Hawking, 33), does not really make sense: the God of Aristotle is not a creator: he chooses nothing and does not "think" nature; he only thinks himself. The same goes for what Hawking has to say about Descartes: he disregards the Cartesian thesis of the "creation of eternal truths," which introduces into the *divine* a sort of "supreme contingency"; for Descartes, God enjoys absolute freedom.

3

The Question of Being
and Creation *Ex Nihilo*

F rom the beginning of Hawking's book, the philosopher experiences an irrepressible sense of uneasiness. True, here the French translation that I am using is partly responsible—but only partly. Stephen Hawking titled his book *The Grand Design*,[1] while the French title, *Y a-t-il un grand architecte de l'univers?* (*Is there a great architect of the universe?*), is an interpretation, and yet it does not betray the true meaning of the book; it simply makes it more explicit. Indeed, God is often seen, in the deism of Freemasonry, as the "Great Architect of the Universe." Similarly, Voltaire confesses:

> *L'univers m'embarrasse et je ne puis songer*
> *Que cette horloge existe et n'ait point d'horloger.*[2]

> [The universe confounds me! I cannot imagine
> such a "watch" without a Watchmaker.]

So be it. But the surprise comes when one realizes that Hawking relates this question to the one Heidegger made the driving force of his philosophical meditation: why is there something rather than nothing?[3] This question, in Heidegger's view, is the most radical of

---

1. The term *design* is obviously used with polemical intent: in the English-speaking world it serves to characterize in a deprecatory way those doctrines that posit an "intelligent design" by God the Creator at the origin of the universe.

2. *Les Cabales* (1772), verses 111–12.

3. Although Hawking correctly formulates this as the "ultimate question" (10), nowhere does he mention his reliance on Heidegger, whose name, unless I am mistaken, is missing from his book.

all questions and therefore opens the way to "first" philosophy. But these two questions, that of the "Great Architect" and that of being, are not identical. To treat them as if they were but one and the same is to confuse the question of the ordering of the world with that of its arising out of nothing. The architect is indeed the one who constructs, that is, who imposes an overall structure on pre-existing elements. He orders, he puts in order, he arranges, he is comparable in many respects to Plato's demiurge, but he does not answer the question: why is there being? This alone is enough to show that Stephen Hawking's enterprise is philosophically ill-advised.

The question so often invoked by Heidegger and taken up by Hawking was articulated first by Leibniz, particularly in *The Principles of Nature and Grace Based on Reason* (1714). After recalling what is termed the "principle of sufficient reason" (nothing is without reason, *nihil est sine ratione*)—of which he is himself the first "formulator"—Leibniz continues: "This principle laid down, the first question which should rightly be asked would be: *Why is there something rather than nothing?* For nothing is simpler and easier than something. Further, suppose that things must exist, we must be able to give a reason *why they must be so* and not otherwise."[4]

It is clear here that the Leibnizian approach occurs in three distinct stages. The first does not consist of the question "why being" because, before asking this question, we must ask ourselves: why ask it?, being (there is something) generally manifesting itself as prime evidence that elicits no "why." For the question to arise, we must first take into account the principle of sufficient reason: if nothing is without reason (first stage), then I can ask myself the question: what is the reason for being of being itself? As Leibniz says, "This principle laid down [that is, the universal principle of sufficient reason], the first question which should rightly be asked would be" the question of being (second stage).[5] Everything therefore starts with the principle of sufficient reason, a principle so little noticed as such (although put into practice by all philosophical thought) that it

4. *Philosophical Works of Leibnitz*, trans. G. M. Duncan (New Haven, CT: Tuttle, Morehouse & Taylor, 1890), 212–13.

5. Ibid.

took, says Heidegger, "two thousand three hundred years . . . before the familiar idea 'Nothing without reason' was expressly posited as a principle and came to be known as a law, recognized in its full import, and deliberately made universally valid."[6] Only then (third stage) can the question of the nature of what is be posed: "Further," says Leibniz, "suppose that things must exist," then we must look for the reason why they cannot be otherwise than they are.[7]

Hawking clearly only considers this last question and does not understand the metaphysical dimension of the question of being. In order to really enter the radical nature of this inquiry, and its extreme difficulty, do we have to attend Heidegger's school and follow the paths of an immense body of work, these "forest paths" that lead nowhere?[8]

We think not. It turns out that the question of the why of the being of things was asked very explicitly a very long time ago (we say the question of being as such, of the "ontological difference," of this sallying forth out of nothing that is realized by being):[9] and that is the very notion of *creatio ex nihilo*. Of course Heidegger rejects this, believing that it annihilates in advance "any questioning of the question (of being)." This notion accepted in faith "can represent no answer at all to [the question of being], because it has no relation to this question. . . . What is really asked in our question is, for faith, foolishness."[10] The reason provided is certainly irrefutable: the notion of *creatio ex nihilo* is irrelevant to the question of being because . . . it is irrelevant! One would have expected something else from such a famous philosopher because, to take the very terms

6. *The Principle of Reason*, trans. R. Lilly (Bloomington, IN: Indiana University Press, 1996), 117–18.

7. *Philosophical Works of Leibnitz*, 213.

8. Heidegger's original German title for his 1950 book, *Holzwege* [Forest Paths], was translated into French as *Chemins qui ne mènent nulle part* [Paths That Lead Nowhere] (Paris: Gallimard, 1962) and into English as *Off the Beaten Track* (Cambridge: Cambridge University Press, 2002).

9. See, in particular, Jean Borella, *Penser l'analogie* (Paris: L'Harmattan, 2012), 42.

10. *Introduction to Metaphysics*, trans. G. Fried & R. Polt (New Haven & London: Yale University Press, 2000), 8. Heidegger forgets that according to Paul (1 Cor. 1:18–4:10), faith is precisely a "foolishness."

in which it is formulated, it is indisputable that the notion of a *creatio ex nihilo* posits the being of what is as being "out of nothing" (*ex nihilo*). And let us not speak of what the no-less-famous physicist Stephen Hawking can tell us about it; it is all too obvious that he is in no position to really perceive its significance.

Going further, we contend that the notion of *creatio ex nihilo* is even the only way to pose, in philosophy, the question of being. And perhaps it is precisely because Leibniz was a Christian that he was led to pose it. Moreover, as we recalled in our book *Penser Analogie* (79), we also find a formulation of this question in the committed creationist Bossuet: "How is it that something is and that nothing can be, if not because being is better than nothing!"[11] True, today the term "creationism" represents no more than a literal and particularly narrow interpretation of the first chapters of Genesis. It is therefore the object of general contempt and its doctrine is degraded, by Christian intellectuals anxious above all to prove their scientific orthodoxy, to the rank of the most ridiculous and inconsistent superstitions. This is a fairly recent and even quite surprising development for philosophers accustomed for centuries to consider this term (independent of the question of transformism) as the designation of a speculatively creditable doctrine. In any case, it is distressing to hear the debilitating as well as aggressive remarks that so many "scientists" make about the deepest and often the most subtle themes of religious philosophy.[12]

But, in some respects, the same could be said of the Heideggerian conclusions. After all, if we ask the question of being, this is because there is being, this is because there is something. If there was nothing, being could not be questioned, and besides, there would be no one to pose the question, nor anyone to ask. In other words, thanks

11. *Élévations sur les mystères* (1694) (Paris: Garnier, 1923), 5–6. Bossuet did not need Leibniz—with whom he corresponded—to formulate the question of being.

12. It would be very useful to read (or reread) the book that Father A.D. Sertillanges, a Dominican Thomist and member of the Institute, a friend of Bergson, devoted to the idea of Creation and its implications for philosophy (*L'Idée de création et son retentissement en philosophie* [Paris: Aubier Editions Montaigne, 1945]), mostly according to the doctrine of St. Thomas Aquinas: astonishment is guaranteed!

to being, it is *out of* being that the question of being can arise. But, in order for being to evoke a question, our reason must be *awakened* to its possible absence: being might not be there. And the awakening of this question is a little too "unnatural" to be able to dispense with the *ex nihilo.*

4

The Being of "There Is"

S till, we must be more specific. For what being is involved here? Is it being as such? But what is being as such? Is it just the idea of being I have in mind when I say "being"? If so, then the question of being, as posed by Leibniz, makes no sense. Whether something is or is not, the idea of being does not change, no more, for example, than does the idea of wealth change if I am rich or poor. The notion of wealth is a question only for someone to whom it can or can not be applied. Thus, Bossuet's formulation makes no sense if one means the "being" of an idea or the concept of being. Actually, in this case, to say that "nothing can be" is to say nothing, since the word "nothing" signifies precisely the absence of being. And, likewise, to ask oneself why there is something and not rather nothing has, formally speaking, no meaning, since by definition "nothing" means precisely that "there is" nothing. However, the word "rather" explicitly establishes a comparison that "nothing" exposes at the same time as impossible. I cannot envision the "there is" of something to compare it to the "there is" of nothing (which the Leibnizian formula supposes), since, by definition, the nothing excludes everything "there is."

In many ways, our conclusions are similar to those of Bergson analyzing the idea of nothingness in *Creative Evolution*. He recognizes first that "existence appears to me like a conquest over nought. I say to myself that there might be, that indeed there ought to be, nothing, and I then wonder that there is something. . . . [In some manner], at first was nothing, and being has come by superaddition to it."[1] But, as soon as we analyze it, we realize that the idea of noth-

1. Trans. A. Mitchell (London: Macmillan and Co., 1922), 291.

ingness comes down to the idea of the absence of one thing by the presence of another that temporarily replaces it. There is only partial or relative nothingness: the nothingness *of* something. Consequently, "the idea of the absolute nought, in the sense of the annihilation of everything, is a self-destructive idea, a pseudo-idea, a simple word."[2] However, although we might understand the idea of nothingness, or rather that of non-being, from the properly metaphysical point of view, we cannot subscribe to the Bergsonian conclusions. All too clearly, whatever may be the relevance of his philosophy (which is incontestable), Bergson seems to "spontaneously" ignore this metaphysical point of view in *Creative Evolution*.

Our purpose in this study is not to consider things from this point of view;[3] so we will say almost nothing about it. We will only point out that it is a bit too hasty to reduce the idea of nothingness to a "simple word." On the one hand, a word is never "simple"; on the other, the notion of "replacing" one thing with another presupposes a "sliding" of things that implies in turn a cosmic vacuum. We challenge anyone to think otherwise: if everything is "full," nothing can move. Not only, as in the sliding puzzle (*jeu de taquin*), is it necessary that there be an empty square to slide the square tokens into and put them in a certain order, but, in addition, the sliding itself and as such can only take place in an empty space. Thus the emptiness, the nought, the nothingness, is like a kind of impossible possibility: it is, in our world, the reflection of Non-being or "More-than-being," the superontological Absolute that overflows all being. This reflection not only accounts for the *game* of the world—as we say, there is "play" in a piece of machinery—but it also accounts as much as possible for this game that is the existence of thought. For every thought is thought of the *possible*, and everything possible, as such, "overflows" being. Thus, if our thought never perfectly fits the being of things, if the *adequatio rei et intellectus*, the adequation of

---

2. Ibid., 299.

3. We did so in *Penser l'analogie*, 89–117. As for the properly cosmological aspect, we have explained this in a new chapter of *Amour et Vérité* (Paris: L'Harmattan, 2011; English translation forthcoming from Angelico Press), 76–104, and will not reiterate it here.

the thing and the intellect, is never perfectly realized (there is always "play"), this is not only due to the imperfection of our knowledge, but this imperfection itself results from the meta-ontological essence of intelligence in its deep and supra-conscious nature. And only this meta- or trans-ontological essence of thought gives meaning, not only to the notion of emptiness (an emptiness obviously never attained in itself, but always as an implicit condition); it also allows for and thereby gives meaning to the notion of being as such, pure and simple being, being as a sought-for and transcendent "object," starting with our implicitly meontological thought in its original source. What we have here is, so to say, a dual "objective-subjective" transcendence, the second referring, in a way, to a transcendence superior to the first.

Having considered all this and returning now to the viewpoint of "physics," we will say that it cannot be a question of being as such, envisaged as a purely abstract idea, but of the being *of something*, of being relative to something, not of "absolute" being. And this is what Leibniz or Bossuet have in mind when they ask the question: why is there something? This question does not open onto infinity. It implicitly presupposes that this involves the being of "things existing in the world," in other words, what Christians call *creation*. And, moreover, language, at least in French, clearly suggests it by this astonishing turn of phrase: *il y a* (there is), or *il n'y a pas* (there is not). The "y" indeed indicates a place, therefore a world, and the turn of phrase signifies an observed presence (of something) in the spatial exteriority taken as a symbol of the "place of all existence," of all "sistence" *out of* (ex), that is, of all *situated* reality, therefore of all conditioned existence. To exist is to be "somewhere," with the understanding that this "somewhere" does not necessarily have the meaning of a physical place, but refers to the position of everything existing in a "world": thus the angels are existing, cosmologically located, although not subject to the spatial condition. This is also the importance of the German *Dasein*, translated in French or English as "existence," literally "there-being," in which, as we know, Heidegger set great store, but in a sense very different from the one considered here. For him there is indeed only one *there*, that is, *a* world, our spatio-temporal universe; whereas we maintain that the idea of a world implies that of a plurality of worlds, none of which are defined by identical conditions, and that the *there* of all existing things simply designates the "worldhood" of its created presence—in other words, its "sistence" both out of nothing and out of God, Who is Being without a *there*, the Non-Situated, the Omnipresent.

And, similarly, the German formulation of "there is," namely "*es gibt*"—literally: "that gives"—indicates that the existent is a given being, a gift of being, a graceful and free outflowing from the Giver of being. And if this given being, or this situated being, poses the question of being, this is because it poses the question of its *own* being, that is, that it might not have been. And why might it not have been? If not for the sole reason that its being (its *esse*) is contingent, that is, it does not possess its own necessity in itself. True, it *is*, as to its own existence, but it is also—and first!—a *created* being. Its contingency marks it negatively as that which is not its own reason for being; its "creativeness" marks it positively as that which is *posited* in being, as that which is granted the grace of being. Standing out of nothing, *ex nihilo*, not only has to do with metaphysics, it is first of all a grace and an honor, the root of all bliss and glory. God has called us to "be."

Thus, neither the "something" nor the "nothing" of the Leibnizian formulation can be taken in the "absolute" sense, which would refer us back to the opposition of being and non-being or, more precisely, of being and nothingness; it would lose its meaning. And, contrary to what Heidegger and Hawking claim, Leibniz's question is philosophically (that is, rationally) viable only in terms of the concept of creation. Otherwise, how not to subscribe to the remark once made by Raymond Ruyer: "Heidegger racks his brains on being like a pythoness on coffee grounds!" Far from being the mere "convenience" spoken of by the German philosopher,[4] faith in the dogma of creation is all that can awaken reason to the mystery of being. The very history of philosophical thought in the West proves it.

---

4. *Introduction to Metaphysics*, 8; an allusion to Montaigne.

5

Laplacian Determinism
and Newtonian Platonism

T he conclusion we have reached, that only the concept of creation *ex nihilo* opens the mind to the mystery of the being of the universe, is clearly opposed to Laplace's response (endorsed by Hawking) to Napoleon's question about God: "God? I do not need this hypothesis."[1] A typical response of a metaphysically infirm intellect, as clearly closed to the mystery of cosmically situated being as to that of its radical origin. This shows once again, if it were necessary, the solidarity of the thought of being with the doctrine of creation. What replaces the "God" hypothesis in Laplace is the thesis of absolute determinism:

> We ought then to consider the present state of the universe as the effect of its previous state and as the cause of that which is going to follow. An intelligence that, at a given instant, could comprehend all the forces by which nature is animated and the respective situation of the beings that make it up, if moreover it were vast enough to submit these data to analysis, would encompass in the same formula the movements of the greatest bodies of the universe and those of the lightest atoms. For such an intelligence nothing would be uncertain, and the future, like the past, would be open to its

---

1. The authenticity of this answer is disputed. It was denied by Laplace himself, according to Jean Largeault, *Principes classiques d'interprétation de la nature* (Paris: Vrin, 1988), 224, n.28. It conveys, however, the general meaning of the Laplacian approach. See the study by Paul Clavier: "La conjonction Kant-Laplace," in *La réception de la philosophie allemande en France aux XIXᵉ et XXᵉ siècle*, ed. Jean Quillien (Lille: Presses Universitaires de Lille, 1994), 50.

eyes. The human mind affords, in the perfection it has been able to give to astronomy, a feeble likeness of this intelligence.[2]

This famous statement (Laplace was not only a great scholar, but also a remarkable writer) is both quite "normal" and quite surprising. It is "normal" inasmuch as it expresses the perfect form of Galilean physics, a neutral framework in which the movements of Newtonian gravitation of the celestial bodies are accomplished. A neutral, empty and completely marginalized framework, since neither space nor time plays any role in the movement of bodies: space and time are mere containers whose nature is not subject to any analysis. Here, Voltaire is right: the universe is a clock; this framework is what is called celestial mechanics, in which there is actually neither past or future, everything is eternally determined by the shape of the pieces of this mechanism, their mutual ordering and the forces they exert on each other. There are no surprises in this universe, everything is always the same. The only mystery that remains is that of the gravitational force that must be interjected, since everything happens as if the bodies were attracted in direct proportion to the product of their masses and in inverse proportion to the square of their distance ($F = GMm/d^2$). This involves, as Newton makes very clear, a mathematization of celestial movements. But as for the nature of this force of gravitation, which is often called gravity, Newton refuses to give an opinion and does not see how to imagine it. Even if it were true that "God said: Let Newton be! And all was light,"[3] what remains is that it is, at heart, only a mathematical description of the universe—one of the most brilliant, to be sure, but which cannot make any pronouncement on either the nature of or the reason for gravitational forces. Newton tells us himself: he considers

---

2. *Philosophical Essay on Probabilities*, Introduction to the second edition (1814), trans. A. I. Dale (New York: Springer-Verlag, 1996), 2.

3. This is the famous epitaph by the poet Alexander Pope (1688–1744): "Nature and nature's laws lay hid in night / God said 'Let Newton be' and all was light."

these forces not physically, but mathematically: wherefore, the reader is not to imagine, that by these words [attractions, impulses, etc.], I anywhere take upon me to define the kind, or the manner of any action, the causes or the physical reason thereof, or that I attribute forces, in a true and physical sense, to certain centers of which I speak (which are only mathematical points); when at any time I happen to speak of centers as attracting, or as endued with attractive powers.[4]

"He could not admit," writes Alexander Koyré, "that matter is able to act at a distance, or be animated by a spontaneous tendency. The empirical corroboration of the fact could not prevail against the rational impossibility of the process."[5] Remember that today the gravitational force remains a mystery, so that the universal principle on which celestial mechanics is based remains unexplained, at least physically, because Newton, unlike Laplace, had perfectly understood that he needed God to *rationally* account for remote interactions:

> To make this system, therefore, with all its motions, required a cause which understood and compared together the quantities of matter in several bodies of the sun and planets, and the gravitating powers resulting from thence . . . and to compare and adjust all these things together in so great a variety of bodies, argues that cause to be, not blind and fortuitous, but very well skilled in mechanics and geometry.[6]

---

4. *Principia* (first edition), book I, trans. A. Motte (New York: Daniel Adee, 1846), 77.

5. *From the Closed World to the Infinite Universe* (Kettering, OH: Angelico Press, 2016), 176. In this respect, the Cartesian concept of vortex physics, that is, of a universe without a void, where everything is filled with "small fragments" of matter, indefinitely divisible and pushing each other by contact, accounts for the gravitation of the stars in a rationally more conceivable way: *Principles of Philosophy*, II, §33–34. Descartes, however, recognizes (§35) that the indefinite divisibility of particles of matter exceeds our understanding. *Principles of Philosophy*, trans. V.R. Miller & R.P. Miller (Dordrecht/Boston/Lancaster: D. Reidel Publishing, 1984), 55–57.

6. *Four Letters from Sir Isaac Newton to Reverend Dr. Bentley*, Letter I; cited in Koyré, ibid., 92.

As we know, absolute space—space in itself, not relative spaces—is defined by Newton as the *sensorium Dei*, that is, as the mode by which God is present to all things, which testifies to Newton's ties to the Cambridge Neoplatonists, especially Henri More.[7]

7. See Jean Zafiropulo and Catherine Monod, *Sensorium Dei dans l'hermétisme et la science* (Paris: Les Belles Lettres, 1975). This book, which goes from Aristotle to Louis de Broglie by way of Newton and Einstein, is a key work. It points out (11) that the expression *sensorium Dei* appears for the first time in Boethius' commentary on Aristotle's *Topics* (8, 5). *Sensorium* is a translation into Latin of the Greek *aïstheterion*, which, in Aristotle, designates what he also calls "common sense." It is the central organ (the heart in Aristotle) that unifies the diversity of the data of the senses to make it *one* object and communicates the awareness of it to the subject. Analogically transposed as the *Dei sensorium*, it refers to the unifying knowledge that God has of the universe, by which He is omnipresent to the world and the world is ontologically present to Him. It is good to recall that much of Newton's work is devoted to alchemy.

6

It Was a Small Ship…

This reappearance of a certain Platonism in the cosmological thought of Europe should not surprise us. It begins in the Renaissance with the recoil from Aristotelian physics, whose death sentence was signed by Galileism. It was also because Aristotle's physics could not account for the movement of a projectile: *a quo moveantur projecta?* ("By what are projectiles moved?") For Aristotle, a body is in motion when another body propels it by contact. How, then, to explain why a thrown body continues its trajectory while no propelling body exerts its action on it? The explanation given by Aristotle (*Physics*, IV, 8, 215a14–18) explains nothing —did he actually believe it?—and aroused the mockery of some ancient commentators, who were well aware of its weakness; likewise, for John Philoponus (sixth century), who proposed what would be called *impetus* physics, studied by many medieval thinkers: it is "a certain incorporeal kinetic force … transmitted by the launcher to the projectile."[1]

But Galileo radicalized the problem. Imagine a ship drawn along by a river current and driven by a uniform movement (that is, at a constant speed). I drop a stone from the top of the mast. Question: where does it fall? At the foot of the mast? Behind the mast? This stone is not launched, it undergoes no *impetus*, it is no longer attached to the movement of the ship; it is simply dropped and abandoned to its own weight, and the mast has moved like the ship to which it is joined. If we follow Aristotle, the stone should fall

---

1. *Joannis Philoponi in Aristotelis Physicorum libros tres priores commentaria*, ed. H. Vitelli (Berlin: Reimer, 1887), 642, 3; quoted by Pierre Pellegrin in his translation of Aristotle's *Physics* (Paris: Flammarion, 2000), 235.

behind the mast since bodies fall in a straight line: in line with the point from which they are released, which point, with the ship advancing, is now behind me. But that is not what happens. The stone falls to the foot of the mast along a straight line perpendicular to the deck of the ship for the one at the top of the mast, but along the obliquity of a parabola for a spectator who would have remained motionless on the river bank. It must therefore be admitted that, although free from any attachment, the stone continued to be animated by the horizontal movement which was its own when I held it at the top of the mast of the moving ship, and secondly that this horizontal displacement was combined with the vertical movement of gravity. In the same way, the moon does not stop falling to the Earth while propelled by its own rectilinear movement that distances it from the Earth; the result is an elliptical orbit. How do we theoretically account for this finding?

Galileo proposes a complete change in understanding the physical design of the movement. For Aristotle, movement is an *effect*: it requires a cause, and it stops when the reason for the movement, that is the end to be realized, is reached. Any movement, whether local movement (displacement in space) or those other forms of movement that are the genesis or corruption of the living—increase or decrease, qualitative change—is a process of realizing the end that moves it. On the contrary, Galileo proposes that we consider movement as a *state*, not as an effect. He no longer needs a cause: a moving body remains in motion, a body at rest remains at rest, except, in the first case, if it encounters an obstacle, and in the second, if it is struck by a moving body. This is called the *principle of inertia*. This is then a conceptual revolution, a new way of looking at things. Mathematically, the gain is considerable; but philosophically, that is, with regard to the true understanding of the phenomenon, the loss is obvious: there is no longer any *raison d'être* for the movement. As the great mathematician René Thom has said, "since the abandonment of Aristotle, physical science no longer knows what it is talking about."[2] Space and time, in Galilean physics, have

---

2. "Aristote et l'avènement de la science moderne: la rupture galiléenne," in M.A. Sinaceur (ed.), *Penser avec Aristote* (Paris: Erès, 1991), 489–94.

become empty containers that have nothing to do with the movements of the bodies that occur in them, and science "is content" to describe things mathematically. Hence Heidegger's (truly untenable) remark: "science does not think."[3]

It could be shown that Galilean physics already implies, in reality, the relativity of space and time, according to Einstein's theory of special relativity.[4] The example we have chosen shows it: there is no absolute description of the trajectory of a falling stone; it depends on the reference point from which it is observed. Moreover, the experience of a rock dropped from a ship's mast is almost superfluous. As the earth turns upon itself (and perhaps around the sun), any body that falls, released from its point of attachment, remains in solidarity with the rotational movement of the Earth that was its own before falling: for an extra-terrestrial, its trajectory would not be vertical, any more than would be that of a bomb dropped by an airplane to an observer on the ground. Similarly, a bird flying in the sky, free of any attachment, is in fact in solidarity with the rotational movement of the Earth on itself. And so for all movements.

Indeed, the nature of a movement can be determined, as to its form, direction, or speed, only in relation to a supposedly motionless space. When we represent the trajectory of the Moon or the Earth, we spontaneously imagine an immobile plane in relation to which only this displacement can have a meaning. But where is this plane? Nowhere. In other words, absolutely speaking, and from a strictly "material" vantage point, the movement of a celestial body does not make sense. And this is true for any body: as Zeno of Elea showed, the arrow is not where it was, it is not where it will be; it is where it is, and therefore it does not move. The only possibility of rationally conferring a real meaning on movement is to suppose it "thought" by God or an angel. It is the angels who "cosmologize" the creation: no angels, no cosmos. This formula will undoubtedly give rise to the contemptuous mirth of modern "conventional wis-

3. *What is Called Thinking?*, trans. F.D. Wieck and J.G. Gray (New York/Evanston/London: Harper & Row, 1968), 8.

4. Cf. Françoise Balibar, *Galilée, Newton lus par Einstein. Espace et relativité* (Paris: P.U.F., 1984).

dom"; it alone, however, meets the demands of philosophy. For, as Ruyer's cosmology establishes, and as we have recalled, following St. Augustine,[5] the unity of each physical element is realized ontologically only in the act that takes cognizance of it, failing which the physical being is reduced to a sheer and "nihilating" dispersal. We must therefore assume a real principle of unity. At the metacosmic and divine level, this is what Plato calls an *Idea*, which is understood by traditional philosophy (St. Thomas Aquinas) as God's knowledge of every physical being. Now, this *Idea* or essence of the thing is "realized" *cosmologically* only in the act of knowledge that a *being of the cosmos* achieves of this physical being. This is the cosmologizing function of the *angelic host* (Sabaoth).

5. *Amour et vérité*, 76–104.

7

No Freedom for
the Friends of Free Will

But physics, as is all too obvious, did not take the path of "angelo-cosmology," or the metaphysical path taken by Newton (and many of his disciples, such as Joseph Rawson); it embarked on the path of mechanical determinism, on the path of mathematical order for which Laplace has given the most complete formulation. This path was "normal," we stated, and we have just seen why. But it is also amazing, if we attentively consider the justification given for it.

Astonishing, yes, when formulated by a declared atheist untroubled in his certainty. It is even surprising that he did not realize that—by imagining his theoretical model of an intelligence embracing the universality of bodies, their respective dispositions and the forces that keep them in order eternally—he had quite simply imagined the "God" hypothesis, a "God" architect, no doubt, not a creator God, but still a kind of God. This "God" is only an observer, he knows the entire and constant order of the universe; basically, this is the ideal projection of a deified human intelligence. In this way a reciprocal game of legitimization is played out between ordered universe and omniscient intelligence: each one vouching for the other. What is eternal, eternally ordered in its constitution and dynamics, is the universe. The omniscient intelligence is presented as the theoretical confirmation of this purely mechanical order, since, as to its own nature, it might possibly be a human intelligence, although infinitely enlarged, and for which therefore this purely mechanical order is supposed to be only an observation. Laplace intends to prove that celestial mechanics is a simple observation, therefore a certain truth, because it would be such for the human intelligence only if it could be omniscient—in other words, if it were God. Now, such a "hypothesis" (which Laplace desperately needs!) betrays (unknowingly?) the spontaneous conception that Laplace and all Laplacians have of human intelligence, that is, the intelligence of an extraterrestrial observer, a being outside of the world, "out of the loop." In other words, the transposing of a merely human intelligence to an all-knowing and all-seeing intelligence is possible because, for Laplace, human intelligence is already, potentially, this transcendent observer who, strictly speaking, actually occupies the place of God.

Nothing is more revealing, in this respect, than the conclusions that materialism—whether Laplacian or not—deems itself entitled to draw from its mechanistic conception. Everything being mathematically regulated in the universe, everything is determined, not only the actions and interactions of celestial bodies, but also the internal and external activity of the earthly bodies, including all the manifestations of human life that we call psychic or spiritual, whereas they are in fact only the product of our organs' functioning, or, for modern biology, the functioning of our cells and their component parts. Thus naturalists, in the nineteenth century, claimed that the brain secretes thought as the liver secretes bile or the kidney urine (Cabanis, Broussais, Vogt, etc.). In our day, Stephen Hawking writes that "Since people live in the universe and interact with the other objects in it, scientific determinism must hold for people as well."[1] As a result, what is called free will is an illusion. "Though we feel that we can choose what we do," writes Hawking, "our understanding of the molecular basis of biology shows that biological processes are governed by the laws of physics and chemistry, and therefore are as determined as the orbits of the planets." Also, "neuroscience supports the view that it is our physical brain ... that determines our actions, and not some agency that exists outside those physical laws."[2] It thus seems that we are only biological machines and our free will only an illusion, an illusion

1. *The Grand Design*, 30.
2. Ibid., 31–32.

resulting from our inability to know the totality of the causes that determine our decisions: their multiplicity defies analysis.[3] Here we are again faced with the opinion of La Mettrie, who in his book *L'Homme-Machine* (1748) argued that "all the faculties of the soul depend so much on the organization of the brain and the whole body that they are obviously only this very organization."[4]

Very well. Thought, consciousness, and the spirit are only epiphenomena of the universal machine's absolute determinism: freedom is an illusion. However, please let a metaphysician ask just one question: La Mettrie, Cabanis, Hawking, and all the others, what are *your* thoughts to *you*? in connection with *your* line of reasoning, with the words *you* utter? Do they express the truth? Without hesitation, you answer: "Certainly!" Now, let us turn to a spiritualist philosopher who advances a contrary line of reasoning. Is his reasoning purely a product of his brain, the functioning of his neurons? "Without a doubt," you say. And your line of reasoning to you, is it purely a product of your neurons? You are obliged by virtue of your own line of reasoning to agree. But then, as much as for the discourse of the metaphysician, your materialistic and deterministic thinking is only an effect of the nature and disposition of your neuronal connections; neither discourse has the least value of truth or makes the slightest sense. And besides, nothing can make sense: meaning has disappeared. The movements of larynx and tongue, the vibrations of the air that they transmit to the eardrum, the transformation of these vibrations into nerve impulses that activate the neuronal structures of the brain: all that is simply the operation of an auditory machine and nothing else. Between two discs with a materialist presentation recorded on one and a spiritualist presentation on the other, which of these discs is right? Not which of these *presentations*, but which of these *discs*—because these presentations are the mere effects of engrams impressed in the wax of each disc, and nothing else. To be right no longer makes sense; for to be right implies that I can aspire to the truth with complete independence, since my thought, my reflection, is not merely a product

3. Ibid., 32.
4. The 1921 edition (Paris: Brossard), 112.

of biological functions. And that is what Laplace, La Mettrie, Cabanis, and Hawking think. They are convinced that they do not think merely according to the multiple determinisms that condition metaphysical thought, whether biological, physicochemical, religious, political, or social. They are free, free to say that there is no freedom. They are out of the loop; they see what is, their words are revelatory for them, but for them alone.

Such is the in fact untenable contradiction of Laplace's or Hawking's attitude. Inevitably, they put themselves in the place of God, themselves men, in order to affirm that all human thought is only the functioning of a machine. In truth, the "agency" to which Hawking denies any appeal is precisely the same one that allows him to deny its reality.

Materialists are like one who counts the number of people in a room and forgets to count himself. However, they have to resign themselves: whether they like it or not, the spirit exists "in complete freedom," we venture to say, essentially obeying only its own nature, whatever else its accidental dependencies might be. And this is precisely what those who extol the materialist thesis *implicitly* and unconsciously affirm as to the *truth* of their thesis, a thesis which, however, *explicitly* denies this. We are reminded here of Pascal's remark that "it will be one of the confusions of the damned to see that they are condemned by *their own reason*, by which they claimed to condemn the Christian religion";[5] condemned not by God, but by their own reason, once death has liberated it from its "sentimental" conditioning and when restored to its original light. Thus atheistic and scientistic materialism would instantly cease to exist as a conviction if it became aware that it unknowingly affirms what it thinks it has denied.

The mere proposal to search for all the factors that condition our choices and decisions, and the possibility of subsequently abandoning this project, given the number of these factors and the complexity of their interactions, implies the freedom of our mind. These multiple conditionings exist—this is undeniable—but the error of the "mechanists" is to imagine the "hypothesis" of freedom as just

5. *Pascal's Pensées*, fragment 562 (New York: Dutton, 1958), 155.

another factor that "spiritualists" would like to insert at the same level as the others, which would, contradictorily, cancel them out, given the significance of the idea of freedom, which precisely evades—and this by definition—the sway of conditioning. But this is not the case. Philosophy shows that ontological freedom is of a different order than that of the horizontal sequence of conditioning factors: it is transcendent to them. Not only does it not contradict them, but it itself conditions their conditioning effectiveness, for otherwise there would be nothing to condition. Freedom is spiritual, and the spirit is freedom. As the German song "Die Gedanken sind frei" puts it, "Thoughts are free,"[6] and they are so in essence; or, better yet, thinking is *itself* freedom. Not to understand this is a kind of mental blindness; not congenital, surely, but a blindness that results from the renunciation of its very own truth by the mind, impressed as it is by the apparently objective determinations of its scientific knowledge: is this not exactly what the gospel calls "sin against the spirit"?

An analogy may give us a further glimpse into what we mean. There seem to be animals, especially insects (bees?),[7] living in a two-dimensional space; in other words, they do not possess the "meaning" of a third dimension. For such beings, an object enclosed in a circle or quadrilateral figure is perfectly elusive: it is found to be in an absolutely closed space. Yet it is enough to "pass" into the third dimension to steal it, which will seem inexplicable to

6. Text and melody in *Lieder der Brienzer Mädchen* (Bern, 1815). But this idea can be traced back to Cicero: "*Liberae sunt . . . nostrae cogitationes*" ("Free are . . . our thoughts"), *Pro Milone*, 29, 79.

7. By observing the dancing of bees (*The Dancing of Bees: An Account of the Life and Senses of the Honey Bee*, trans. D. Isle & N. Walker [New York: Harcourt Brace Jovanovich, 1966]), Karl von Frisch showed that bees "used" a gestural mode of communication to indicate the location and distance to the flowers where they had gathered pollen. However, if the pollen trove was located *vertically* above the bees, they could forage for it but not indicate its location. This inability is a sign that animal intelligence is devoid of the sense of transcendence, the vertical being the realization of transcendence in spatial mode—and man's aptitude for transcendence is the reason why man is the only truly vertical animal. In the same way Christ could not physically manifest his "exit" from the world except according to the mode of ascension. To deny the Ascension is to deny the Incarnation of the Divine Word.

a two-dimensional being. The same is true for the spiritual dimension of human reality. The whole thrust of modern civilization is focused on depriving our minds of the sense of the supernatural, that is, of the perception of this "spiritual dimension," and even on persuading us that to believe in its reality is to sin against reason.

8

Meaning Has Disappeared

The reality of the mind should be obvious, and one experiences a kind of fatigue at having to recall this constantly (and yet without effect...): it is the same here as for someone who denies the existence of light on the pretext of never having seen it, which is perfectly accurate since we only see colors and shapes. Likewise, we do not see or touch the mind, but it is thanks to the mind that we are conscious of seeing and touching. In this case, we want not only to emphasize a glaring, though widely unnoticed, contradiction in the mechanistic thesis, but, more radically and positively, to capture or glimpse something of the reality of the mind. Otherwise, as we have said, the idea that there is meaning disappears: in the strictly materialistic world of the physicist Hawking, as in that of the biologist Jacques Monod and the ethno-sociologist Claude Lévi-Strauss, the idea that there might be *meaning* no longer makes sense. Meaning is no longer possible; the *reality* of "meaning" has disappeared, which these scholars seem to be unaware of with regard to the truth-value they attribute to their own writings.

Thus Levi-Strauss, though of a more philosophical bent than many such figures, asserts that "meaning always results from the combination of elements that are not themselves significant." Hence it follows that "meaning is always reducible ... behind all meaning, there is nonsense, and the opposite is not true."[1] Extrapolating from this thesis, in *The Naked Man* he offers us a radical theory according

1. "Réponses à Paul Ricœur," in *Esprit* (November, 1963), 637. The reduction of meaning to nonsense, that is, to what is not a meaning (but a thing), has been brilliantly supported by the "Vienna Circle" (*Wiener Kreis*), a group of philosophers and mathematicians who, shortly after 1925, founded what is called *positivism* or *logical empiricism*, according to which a language, a proposition has meaning only

to which the structures of the language, like those of cultural and religious systems, are reduced to the structures of the macromolecules of deoxyribonucleic acid composing the genetic "code" (DNA): these systems consist, "at the outset, of a finite group of discrete units, chemical bases or phonemes, themselves devoid of meaning, but which, when variously combined into units of a higher rank[2]—the words of language or triplets of nucleotides— specify a definite meaning or a definite chemical substance."[3] As we have shown in *The Crisis of Religious Symbolism*,[4] meaning's reality on this model is the most implausible, the most inexplicable, the most miraculous of appearances, compared to which the so-called "superstitions" of the Christian faith are models of rationality. We are awash in "magic" here, just like the scientistic mythology that speaks of genetic code as an objective reality, whereas it is in fact a metaphor, to be handled with caution and whose validity is most uncertain. Moreover, a critical study of Lévi-Strauss's vocabulary easily reveals its extreme inaccuracy: how can one speak of "higher

---

as "designatable," and this meaning can be reduced by a process of empirical designation. If we cannot indicate in physical experience what words or propositions mean, they have no meaning. There is no need to appeal to metempirical "realities" to account for the world. "The scientific conception of the world," says the School, "is not only free from metaphysics, but directed against it" (*Manifeste du Cercle de Vienne et autres écrits: Carnap, Hahn, Neurath, Schlick, Waismann, Wittgenstein*, ed. Antonia Soule [Paris: P.U.F, 1985], 113). Leszek Kolakowski has traced the history of this current, from Ockham to Russell, in *La Philosophie positiviste*, trans. [Polish to French] Claire Brendel (Paris: Denoël-Gonthier, 1977). See also Louis Vax, *L'Empirisme logique* (Paris: P.U.F., 1970). This doctrine can be summarized in the following proposition: "The propositions of logic . . . are tautologies" (they all say the same thing), that is to say, "nothing"; Wittgenstein, *Tractatus Logico-Philosophicus*, 6.1 and 6.11, trans. C.K. Ogden (London: Kegan Paul / New York: Harcourt, Brace, 1922), 76– 77.

2. Translator's note: The English translation neutralizes the point argued by the author below. Therefore a literal translation of the original French—*unités de rang supérieur*—is retained here; the English rendering is: "combined into *more complex units*."

3. *The Naked Man: Introduction to a Science of Mythology*, vol. 4, trans. J. and D. Weightman (London: Jonathan Cape, 1981), 685.

4. Jean Borella, *The Crisis of Religious Symbolism* (Kettering, OH: Angelico Press /Sophia Perennis, 2016), 282–83.

rank" in a structuralist system which, by definition, ignores any principle of hierarchization? This is why, in the case of this mechanistic atheism, we are entitled to speak of "deception."

In philosophy, this deception has been particularly highlighted and combatted by Raymond Ruyer: while rejecting many of his views, we have mainly learned about the philosophy of nature from his—hardly known—work.[5] Ruyer also joins the English philosopher and mathematician Whitehead, often quoted by Wolfgang Smith,[6] in his condemnation of "Cartesian bifurcationism," that is, a doctrine that offers a false dichotomy between thinking reality and extended reality, before which we can only "bifurcate," turning to either one or the other alternatively depending on the case. Ruyer's great strength, besides his speculative genius, is to speak of the reality of things, and not be content, like the vast majority of contemporary philosophers, to speak as philosophy speaks. From this point of view, Ruyer, like Whitehead, is right to argue that, with regard to the concern for truth, there is not, or should not be, a difference between science and philosophy.

---

5. *Problème de gnose* (Paris: L'Harmattan, 2007), 131–141, cf. *infra*, footnote 3 on page 120.

6. *Ancient Wisdom and Modern Misconceptions* (Kettering, OH: Angelico Press/ Sophia Perennis, 2015), 19–21.

9

Why Is Science
Officially Atheistic?

W e have to wonder why such a glaring deception is so little recognized, despite the work of some of the greatest philosophers in the West.[1] Why is this atheistic and materialistic determinism alone entitled to be heard and understood, celebrated and admitted as definitive truth by the great majority of the public, drawing religion in this way into the discredit of metaphysics? Ruyer suggests that the "religious crisis of our time" is due to the "unbelievable nature of religious mythologies," which he intends to supersede with what he calls the "Princeton gnosis."[2] At first sight, this view seems incontestable. But, taking a closer look, one perceives its insufficiency. The debate between a certain scientific rationality and religious faith is not of present-day origin. Christian revelation, over the course of 1,700 years, lived with the ideas of philosophers and scientists, if not on good terms, at least without complete mutual rejection, except in rare instances. Without mentioning the exemplary work of St. Thomas Aquinas, let us

1. Most notably Raymond Ruyer, Henri Bergson, and Etienne Gilson.
2. *La gnose de Princeton* (Paris: Hachette Littérature, 1977), 15. Ruyer, in this book, presents himself as the "secretary" for a group of American scientists who would be the true authors of this "gnosis." In fact, and except for the repercussions provoked by Ruyer's book, he is himself the author of this "vision of the world," a scientific-religious (but non-Christian) vision that he had already set forth in several of his previous works. To differentiate this gnosis, he had vacillated over using the name of several universities, especially Princeton and Pasadena. We have given a detailed analysis of Ruyerian gnosis in *Problèmes de gnose* (Paris: L'Harmattan, 2007), 113–212.

recall that Copernicus was a canon and dedicated his *De revolution-ibus orbium celestium* to Pope Paul III, who accepted this dedication; that Galileo was a believer; that Descartes made a pilgrimage to Our Lady of Loreto and strove to show the agreement of his physics with the dogma of Eucharistic transubstantiation; that Malebranche was a priest of the Oratory; and that Leibniz, one of the most universal geniuses that the world has known, recognized the alliance of "theology and ethics with reason."[3] Atheism would become socially important only in the eighteenth century.

So it is not science, in its various revolutions, which has made "religious mythology" unbelievable, as much as the progress in material techniques that seem to attest to the truth of this science in the eyes of all. Science alone could not achieve this: in any case, the principles of Galilean or post-Galilean physics, as we briefly recalled, were not always easy to understand and their cosmological implications could not be truly appreciated by the general public. And, although this pertains to a now-obsolete idea of the world, it is not even certain that they are appreciated today by all our contemporaries: our universe, in reality, is no longer Newtonian, but Einsteinian and quantum. While the miracles of steam, electricity, atomic energy, molecular biology, computing, telecommunication, etc., are both spectacular and indisputable, is this all? No, because ultimately these technological miracles must also be borne along by an atheistic science, or otherwise the feats of modern technology will gradually lose their miraculous character and become commonplace to the extent they are available for our daily use. But when an expert peremptorily asserts, alluding to theories quite poorly understood by the vast majority of people, that religion is a useless superstition and that "God is dead," we think we understand very well what this means and give credence to such a statement, surely proven, it is believed, by extraterrestrial navigation, heart transplants, and television. We understand it very well because we know, or think we know, what religion is.

3. *New Essays Concerning Human Understanding*, trans. A.G. Langley (New York & London: Macmillan, 1896), 66.

The question that needs to be asked is therefore: Why has science become atheist? Why has Galilean-Newtonian physics led, notwithstanding the faith of its founders and the religious convictions of Kepler, Descartes, Pascal, Leibniz, and so many others, to the "death of God"? Are rules rationally derived from the principles of this physics—rules as yet unnoticed by the founders—solely responsible for this?

We think not. The sources of scientific atheism are certainly manifold, and each must be considered individually. However, we will venture to distinguish three sources (among others), three which are more or less interdependent, to the point that it is hardly possible to rank them by importance.

There is certainly a critical reaction to and ultimately a rejection of a Church that history seems to have charged with crimes and whose authority seems more and more unbearable. Thus Diderot "liked to relate the words of a friend before a painting of Christ's flagellation: 'Strike and strike hard. Only a few drops of blood for all those his accursed religion will shed.'"[4] The cause of atheism is joined to the anti-Christian cause and is justified by it. The struggle against Christ, against his priests, joins the fight for justice and freedom. Atheists are primarily "libertines" in the seventeenth-century sense, not primarily licentious and immoral, but "free thinkers," opponents of any limitation to the freedom to think: it is doctrinal libertinism. In a work published in 1623, *Questiones celeberrimae in Genesim* (a commentary on Genesis), Father Mersenne estimates that the number of atheists in Paris alone was 50,000.[5] This atheism assumes some sort of intellectual hegemony in the eighteenth century. It becomes the attitude required to appear intelligent and to salve one's conscience about the obscurantism of a church deemed intolerant. There is therefore, in this atheism, a feeling of hatred towards God and His ecclesiastical representatives.

---

4. Quoted by Michel Delon, *Diderot* (Paris: Gallimard, 2004), 106.

5. René Taveneau, *Le catholicisme dans la France classique*, vol. 1 (Paris: Société d'édition d'enseignement supérieur, 1980) considers this estimate "unverifiable and surely excessive" (252).

But with this feeling of hatred is mixed a sense of pride, a pride that arouses the certainty of knowing how to reduce the enigma of the universe to mathematical formulas, and thus to dominate and master it. Now it is the universe itself, the mystery of earthly things in their manifold varieties, and that of heavenly bodies in their eternal gravitations, that are the primary sources for religious mythologies and their retinue of superstitions. To pierce this mystery, to cast the light of reason on the intelligible order of the world: this is simultaneously to make religions and superstitions fade away and to promote human understanding to the position of commander-in-chief of reality, and therefore to that of God: the "God" hypothesis becomes useless. Here we have the second cause of atheistic domination. All this is well known and quite commonplace.[6]

6. An exemplary illustration of these themes can be found in the famous book by Charles François Dupuis, "Citoyen Français," *Abrégé de l'Origine de tous les cultes* (Paris: chez H. Agasse, Imprimeur-Libraire, An VI de la République). Dupuis displays a great (not always very reliable) erudition in the *Abrégé* [abridgement] of his *Origine des tous cults* (1794, 12 volumes) to prove that all religions go back to the adoration of the stars and forces of the universe. It is a pantheistic materialism. Its reading is not without interest.

10

Idealist Blocking and the
Realism of Substantial Form

The Idealistic Interpretation of Quantum Physics:
Still a Prisoner of Cartesian Bifurcationism

A less trivial question helps us identify a third cause of scientific atheism, and this is the question: what gave rise to the now-regnant mechanistic and materialistic conception of the universe, and therefore to the rejection of any metaphysical interference in the field of physics? For it is not enough to recognize in the advent of modern science the cultural occasion for putting an end to religious mythologies; one must still ask: why this advent? This also amounts to asking: why have the metaphysical principles of ancient philosophy—thanks to which, as we have recalled, many great minds thought they could "think" religion and agree more or less with its dogmas—ceased to be valid? Why did philosophers lose their capacity for speculative thought? Why such a radical change of *episteme*, that is, an epoch's general idea about scientific knowledge (as understood by Michel Foucault)?

Genuinely answering this question—if it can be answered at all—exceeds the scope of this reflection. We would only like to draw attention to one point, but an essential one, which we consider the major *philosophical* cause of so-called scientific atheism: the abandonment or rejection, by the new philosophy, of the notion of *substantial form*,[1] an Aristotelian and scholastic notion, a key (along

---

1. The notion of substantial form is not far removed from the Ruyerian notion of "absolute overflight [French: *survol*]," or even from "elementary consciousness" (even if Ruyer had little sympathy for Aristotle), provided that the term "overflight" is not given the "spatial" meaning that it seems to suggest: this overflight is immanent to what it flies over. *Neofinalism*, trans. A. Edlebi (Minneapolis: University of

with the notions of potency and act) to ancient cosmology, but which alone would enable us to think rigorously about quantum reality. In the absence of this key, some of the greatest contemporary physicists think themselves obliged to favor a kind of idealism, the contrary option, realism (that is, the reality value of our scientific concepts), seeming to be *impossible*. Such is the case, for example, with Schrödinger (but not with Whitehead, who is a realist), who writes in *My View of the World*: everything "happens in our experience of the world, without [our] ascribing to it any material substratum as the object of which it is an experience."[2] Just as Laplace does not need the "God" hypothesis, Schrödinger, relying on a certain interpretation of the *Vedanta*, does not need the "external material world" hypothesis. For, in the seventeenth century, it was actually "religious mythology" that was made "unimaginable" by the advent of mechanistic physics, just as today, by a strange reversal of things, it is quantum reality, the world presented to us by wave mechanics, which has become "unthinkable and unimaginable," at least to the extent that we think of any bodily reality as able to be localized in a given place. Now—and this is basically the fundamental difficulty with quantum physics—quantum "beings" cannot be located at a given point in the electromagnetic field of their possible appearance; they are as it were in several places in space at the same time: "It is not enough to say that it is impossible to know the exact position and velocity of a particle simultaneously. It must be maintained that, in general, there is no such thing as a well-determined position or velocity. Matter and light become fugitive indeed, and any hope of representing the world in terms of pictures and motions becomes nothing more than an empty dream."[3] The two physicists who signed this statement were students of Louis de Broglie (who prefaced their work); like him, they did not totally refrain from searching for a "realistic" epistemology, in terms of bodily representations.

Minnesota, 2016), chap. 9. [TRANS. NOTE:] In Alyosha Edlebi's English translation, *survol* is rendered as "domain of survey."

    2. Trans. C. Hastings (Cambridge: Cambridge University Press, 1983), 67.

    3. J.L. Andrade e Silva and G. Lochak, *Quanta*, trans. P. Moore (London: World University Library, 1969), 164.

We cannot repeat here what we have ex-plained in *Amour et Vérité*,[4] but we would only like to stress that the "idealistic" conclusion to which Schrödinger (like many others) thinks himself necessarily led, and which goes as far as a kind of negation of the outside world, remains in fact captivated by the bifurcationism denounced by Whitehead. If indeed one has the choice between physical matter and thinking substance (the *res cogitans* of Descartes), then, since the experimental data of microphysics is not representable in terms of material reality, one can only opt for the reduction of the world to the mental mode of its representation. We are obviously at the antipodes of Laplacian mechanics—its universe has completely collapsed—but we have not left behind the bifurcationist dichotomy and therefore the way Laplacian materialism posed the problem.

Reality of Substantial Form

How does the notion of substantial form—a notion vilified and despised by Laplacian materialism as well as Schrödinger's idealism, classed as it is with others, such as "entelechy" or "life force," in the "muddle" of Aristotelianism's (fictitious and useless) entities,[5]— how does this notion, if not decide, at least allow a conceivable meaning to be given to what Wolfgang Smith calls the *quantum enigma*?[6] A brief historical review is in order here.

The form (*forma* in Latin, *morphe*, *eïdos* or *logos* in Greek) is what "informs" in the active sense of the verb: that which "gives a form" to some matter which, by itself, is deprived of it. Everything in the sublunary world is composed of a form and some matter. The "matter" (which is not necessarily of a bodily nature) is therefore "what" the form informs. In itself the form, in Aristotle's sense, is structure, organization, intelligible unity, the principle of activity for a being on which it confers a unity and an identity. Does this not necessarily involve, therefore, the spatial envelope or *shape* of a body?

---

4. *Amour et Vérité*, 76–104.

5. *My View of the World*, 67. This view is shared by most current philosophers.

6. See W. Smith, *The Quantum Enigma: Finding the Hidden Key* (San Rafael, CA: Angelico Press/Sophia Perennis, 2011).

But the form-envelope is obviously the effect of a structuring and specifying form. Thus the form "Apollo" informs the marble of a statue. It is not of a spatial nature, since it exists not only in the marble of the statue to which it confers its identifiable figure but also in the mind of the sculptor whose movements it guides, as well as in the religious culture of Greece which provides the prototype. But suppose the marble of the statue, say Paros marble, is also composed of a form (a specific "Paros" form, to be distinguished from a specific "Carrara" form) and a material, marble in general, which is in turn composed of form and matter: the form "marble" and the matter "stone," and so on, according to a regression which leads us to a matter less and less "informed," a kind of ontological residue, the "that-from-which" all things are made, and which, being below all forms, is not accessible to knowledge, since it is always the form which makes it possible to identify a thing, to recognize it. Form is what confers a thing's species and intelligibility. The ultimate matter or *materia prima* is therefore unintelligible, being deprived of form: it is at the limit of existence. Thus, it is the form that gives a thing its being, outside of which the thing is only a possibility of being.

Substantial form is to be distinguished from *accidental* form: substantial form is that which lets the compound exist as *one* substance, that is, *an* individually distinct being (in-dividuus means "what is not divisible"), while the accidental form introduces, into the already substantially formed compound, only secondary and non-ontologically composed modifications, for instance the color (accidental form) with which one can paint a piece of wood. Thus the substantial form cannot be isolated, as to its reality, from the matter which it informs; it is in the compound (which as such cannot be decomposed except in the abstract) that its existence can be deduced. In the formulation of Thomas Aquinas: "Just as substantial form does not have existence in itself, separately from that to which it comes, neither does that to which it comes, namely, matter."[7] But this cannot mean that form is, in itself, of a corporeal or

---

7. *Aquinas on Being and Essence: A Translation and Interpretation by Joseph Bobik* (Notre Dame, IN: University of Notre Dame Press, 1965), 239.

spatial nature. Space, and therefore the corporeal, insofar as it is viewed according to the spatial mode of its existence, is indefinitely divisible; consequently, it is impossible to find, in this corporeal space, an indivisible unity. Therefore, the unity and individuality of any being, whether it is *a* man, *a* cat, or *a* tree, *a* cell, *a* molecule, *an* atom, or *a* corpuscle—the individuality required by reason (a being that is not *a* being is not a *being* either)—cannot be assured "materially": it is necessarily of a transpatial nature. And this applies to all bodily beings, whether molecules or atoms. How do we account for the unity of an atom? How do we explain that the uranium atom is "formed," when it is formed as a "planetary" structure of ninety-two electrons (which have no material support) orbiting a nucleus, while the hydrogen atom has only one electron orbiting the nucleus? What guides the formation of these structures defined by the precisely ninety-two existing "atomic" types which, therefore, are somehow pre-existent to their physical realization?

Whether the "uranium form" or the "hydrogen form," forms that are permanent "possibles," such forms constitute the first, substantial, ontological reality of their transient physical realization. Not being, in themselves, subject to the spatial condition, to a *partes extra partes* spreading out, these forms account for the organization, the unitary structuring of electronic elements which appear to us spatially distinct from each other (otherwise, how do we count them?), while ordering each other in a rigorous contemporaneity, as if an invisible hand guided them and held them *together*. And this would be even more striking if we considered the formation of an organ or a living being. The formation of an eye or a bone is not accomplished in a series of successive steps, but synergistically, by the concordant building-up of elements distant from each other, but which work together, at the same time and all with a single end in view. The form "bone" or "eye" is not "above" the biological material; it is immanent to this material, or rather this material is only the mode of spatialization of the form, in itself non-material. Thus, a corpse is not a body minus its soul; for corporeal reality, there is only the living body. At the moment when life disappears, the reality of the body changes, the cells immediately *disintegrate* [French: *défont*, unmade], proof that the living cells are *made*

[French *font*] continuously: as we said at the beginning, the form is an informative *activity*.

The Triple Nature of the Form

What is the nature of this form? Traditional philosophy teaches us that it is of a "psychic" nature or, alternatively, of a subtle or animic nature. We are in fact directly aware of what the "psychic" is. A field of consciousness, for example the view I have of my room, provides us with the model of a reality whose multiple elements are related to one another in a single act of consciousness without my having to go from one to another to bring them together. This is just a model, but the only one available to us. It allows us, however, to posit a "soul" in things,[8] a soul endowed not with a reflective consciousness, but an elementary "consciousness,"[9] an animic principle of unitary organization, not only in living beings, but even in the most basic physical realities, as we are invited to do by the data of quantum physics. Actually, it is an illusion, the fruit of an objectifying conceptualization of our sensible knowledge, to believe that we live in an entirely spatial corporeal world, entirely spread out before us. We live in a universe whose objective and unmistakable consistency is of a psycho-corporal nature, and even more.

For we are experiencing a third type of reality in addition to the corporeal and the psychic: the reality of a spiritual nature, the most common example of which is provided by our intellectual representations, particularly in mathematics and metaphysics. If the corpo-

---

8. "*In* things" has only a rhetorical value here: the "souls" in question do not exist inside things as in a container, they are the things themselves. This entire analysis is inspired by Ruyer's lectures, particularly chapter 9 of his masterwork, *Neofinalism*.

9. The expression "primary *consciousness*" as used by Ruyer is not without its drawbacks, mainly that of returning almost invariably to our experience of a *reflective* and therefore dualizing consciousness: all consciousness of something (object) is virtually conscious of self as conscious (subject). But it also has the advantage of providing us with the only analogical model of a knowledge immanent to its cognitive being. See Ruyer's *La conscience et le corps* (Paris: P.U.F., 1950).

real, considered in itself, is "spatialist"; if the psychic, considered in itself, is "temporalist" (life is in time); the spiritual or realm of semantics,[10] the realm of essences, intelligible realities, is outside of time: it is "essentialist and actualist." In its loftiest, most truly metaphysical mode, form is identified with essence and finally with the archetype, of which it is the cosmological mode inasmuch as it is not only a "thing," as the use of the noun (the form) might lead us to believe, but also an informative activity.

There are many other things to consider. A more complete account can be found in a chapter from my book *Amour et Vérité* entitled "Le détour cosmologique." We have said enough, however, to catch a glimpse of the third cause we indicated that accounts for the abandonment, in the eighteenth century, of any reference to traditional philosophy, that is, to notions of form and matter, potency and act, essence and existence, and hence of God, the creator and ruler.

This cause obviously lies in the rejection of these metaphysical principles. But if we rejected them—and this is the point we were coming to—it was because we were no longer able to perceive the truth. What occurs in the eighteenth century is an almost general diminution of the metaphysical capacities of European intelligence. For these notions were previously accepted as rationally and intellectually obvious, provided that one apply one's mind to them, whatever the divergent interpretations given by philosophers and scholars. But, and probably because of the attention devoted exclusively to the mathematical reduction of the world, the light they brought was no longer accepted: in truth, we were no longer able to understand them, they were no more than empty words.

What of today, though? Many physicists who are trying to take into account the recently revealed mystery of "dark matter" announce that we are at the dawn of a major cosmological revolu-

---

10. Semantics does not refer here to considerations about human language. It designates a real metaphysical being whose nature is to be a meaning, that is, an intelligible.

tion.[11] However, the Einsteinian theory of general relativity raises many questions. Perhaps the human mind will be led to rediscover the meaning of Scripture where it tells us that "in the beginning God created the heavens and the earth."

11. It seems, according to the most recent hypotheses, that the atomic organization of matter (nucleus and peripheral electrons) as defined by quantum mechanics constitutes at most only five percent of cosmic reality. The remaining ninety-five percent would consist of a "matter" whose *non-atomic* organization is completely unknown to us. Note also that the image of an atom consisting of a nucleus and peripheral electrons is only a mathematically based theoretical model, and is not illustrative of the atom's "spatial" reality, which is undepictable.

11

The God of Reason
and the Grace of Faith

God as a Question of Reason

All too briefly, we have shown the things left unsaid, the mis-understandings and gaps in knowledge of what is rightly called scientistic materialism: from the philosophical point of view its rejection of "God" must be seen as "feeble-minded." It is understood that the term "God" is here only indicative and other designations may be preferred: Supreme Being, Eternal, First Principle, Absolute, etc. Granted, this diversity of names may point to very different "theologies" and metaphysics. But, beyond their disparities, these "theologies" are oriented towards the recognition of a "Something" transcendent to the world. This recognition—and this is the major point—is not a matter of religious faith, but a *rational* certainty. It is, moreover, a constant dogma of the Catholic Church, defined in particular at the First Vatican Council, that "God, the beginning and end of all things, can be known with certitude by the natural light of human reason from created things,"[1] which means that this knowledge requires neither revelation nor grace, although it obviously does not exclude them.

We are thinking here of the question of the demonstration of the existence of God, a demonstration illustrated by many famous philosophical approaches. A clarification is needed. It would be a mistake, in our opinion, to consider that these demonstrations are

---

1. From the translation of "Constitutio De Fide Catholica" in *The Vatican Council and its Definitions*, ed. Cardinal Henry E. Manning, 2nd ed. (New York: D. & J. Sadler, 1871), 210.

intended to *produce* the certainty of God's existence (or rather of His reality, for God does not exist in the way a creature does) as a cause *produces* its effect; the reality of God cannot depend on a demonstration. Rather, these facilitate an *awareness of the rational nature* of belief in God, a realization necessitated by the fact that it was first the received faith that spoke of God, no human society having lived without religion. "God"—or whatever name is bestowed on Him—was first of all what religions have taught to the children of men. From this comes, in modern societies that separate the religious from other cultural phenomena, the spontaneous tendency to regard the question of God's existence as a matter of faith and not science. However, on closer inspection, the validity of such a categorization is likely to be rejected, despite appearances and common opinion. This is in fact because the *question* of God's existence is not first posited by the act of faith; it is posited, eventually, only by a second act of reason. Clearly the person of faith believes in the existence of the God to Whom he speaks; at least that is an objective observation made from the outside by someone who thinks rationally about this belief. But the act of faith consists practically, not in overcoming a doubt as to the existence of the invisible Being that is God, but in trusting what God has revealed through His Church. In reality, the explicitly formulated notion of existence, with regard to God, is inseparable from its being called into question and only comes to the fore when it is questioned: philosophy, as Plato and Aristotle teach us, is always the daughter of wonder. And questioning is properly an act of reason that asks itself: how is it possible to believe? Faith, therefore, in human terms, comes first and precedes the questionings of reason.

This is not to say, however, that the act of faith is reduced to a maneuver of the will alone, more or less sentimental in nature, or that it is purely a product of education, a kind of societal conditioning. As great as the strength of the religious education received might be, it cannot act without a more-or-less conscious, more-or-less vigorous acquiescence of reason. And this is true even in a child. This involvement can go almost unnoticed, but it is always present and always ends up manifesting itself. It will be objected, no doubt, that historical and indeed everyday experience shows the opposite, and that a person or a community can be made to believe in the most false and dangerous ideas. This is undeniable. But, besides the fact that such persuasion utilizes all sorts of means to annul the resistances of reason (and thus presupposes precisely its presence in the sought-for acceptance), it also makes a case for the *reasons* that ground and justify its ideology: to deceive reason is not to deny it, it is to suppose its presence. The possibility of deception only proves that reason (*ratio* means calculation), which is the properly human faculty of logically ordering our thoughts according to the norms of first principles (non-contradiction, identity, excluded middle, causality, etc.), is fallible, not in itself, but because the knowledge on which it works comes from outside itself (in itself reason *knows* nothing), that is, comes from the intellect that is fundamentally the "sense" of the real, whether sensible or intelligible. Now the intellect apprehends a reality only on the condition that this *appears* before it, whether sensorially or intellectually, and according to this appearance. But everyone knows that appearances can be deceiving. It is not the intellect that is mistaken a priori: like the eye, it sees what it sees and has no other mode of knowledge. But it can be deceived, or its power of vision can be altered or limited, and even almost nil. The work of reason, therefore, does not consist in perceiving better than intellect what the intellect gives it to know, but in judging its validity (and therefore its truth) according to the coherence of the overall data. Its work is always secondary and dependent.[2]

From this point of view demonstrations of God's existence are useful and even necessary. Since reason is present in every act of faith, this presence must be taken into account and exercised if it is to develop as completely as possible. The questioning of the exist-

---

2. Reason is understood here in its specific, analytical, discursive and combinatorial activity. But the term can be taken in a broader sense, as synonymous with thought, mind, or intelligence. Thus, Augustine speaks of a "higher reason" in the sense of contemplative intelligence, and a "lower reason" (*ratio inferior*) in the sense of ratiocinative reasoning (*De Trinitate*, XII, 15). St. Thomas Aquinas accepts the Augustinian distinction, clearly marking the difference between intellect (or higher reason) and ratiocinative reason, but strongly maintains that both belong to the same power of the soul (*Summa theologiae*, I, q. 79, a. 9).

ence of God offers reason the highest exercise that it can perform, one that nothing else is able to offer. But the demonstration of the rationality of the idea of God is not for the sole purpose of justifying reason in its participation in the act of faith—reason is not insane in acquiescing to the reality of "He Who is"—it also leads the intellect to a greater profundity in thinking about God. Every demonstration of the existence of God reveals something of His essence.

God is Known by Unknowing

However, as rational as our recognition of God's existence might be, we do not go so far as to make God a "being of reason." The God of thought is thought of as something that eludes thought. Surely we have here one of the reasons atheism will use to justify its rejection of such an object of thought: when we think of God, we do not know what we are thinking, and we know we do not know. Now St. Thomas Aquinas also says this in the clearest but also the most profound way: to know that we do not know what we think when we think of God is "the ultimate and most perfect limit of our knowledge in this life," as Dionysius says in *Mystical Theology*.[3] "We are united with God as the *Unknown*. Indeed, this is the situation, for, while we know of God what he is not, what He is remains quite unknown [*manet penitus ignotum*]. Hence, to manifest his ignorance of this sublime knowledge, it is said of Moses that he went *to the dark cloud wherein God was* (Exodus 20:21)."[4]

Actually, if the thought of a known-as-unknown God is what leads our thought to its ultimate and most perfect "pitch" of knowledge, this is because of a crucial truth: a limit is experienced only when we are compelled to attempt an impossible surpassing, to have the experience of an unbreachable transcendence. Our thinking is somehow overwhelmed by the thought of God: God imposes

3. Pseudo-Dionysius, *Mystical Theology*, I, §3. In *Pseudo-Dionysius: The Complete Works*, trans. Colm Luibheid (New York/Mahwah, NJ: Paulist Press, 1987), 136–37. See also Jean Borella, *Lumières de la théologie mystique* (Lausanne: L'Age d'homme, 2002), 47–117.

4. *Summa contra Gentiles*, III, 49, 9; in *On the Truth of the Catholic Faith*, trans. V. J. Bourke (Garden City, NY: Doubleday, 1956), 170.

Himself on our thought as That which it can not encompass.[5] Such is, we believe, one of the meanings of what is called, since Kant, the "ontological argument," for which St. Anselm gave the decisive formulation and which Descartes took up, in his own way, no less brilliantly.[6] This speculative experience of the *limit*—the possibility of this experience to be found only in the idea of God—is less easy to carry out than current atheism, even of a philosophical bent, imagines; according to Pascal's remark: "atheism shows strength of mind, but only to a certain degree."[7] Having the intellectual experience of His insurmountable transcendence is not enough of a reason for rejecting the idea of God. Quite the contrary: only when faced with this transcendence do we experience the transparency of this "idea of God," which lets itself be traversed by thought without the latter encountering any other resistance than that of its own speculative inconsistency, the atheist being convinced that he knows what this "idea" is all about. So he thinks he can easily deconstruct it (in various ways, according to the kind of atheism), while the believer is doing exactly the opposite, so that we are faced with this paradox: it is the atheist who thinks he knows perfectly well what he is thinking when he speaks of "God," whereas the believer, to the extent he deepens his awareness of the idea of God, progresses more and more towards what Evagrius of Pontus has called "infinite ignorance."[8] Progressing more and more, yes, because he must abandon all his *false knowings* of God, false not so much in themselves—for all such knowings are relatively true—as in the illusion where thought is found to be imprisoned by this knowledge.

---

5. We find in "Scottish philosophy" (between 1750 and 1850)—that of Thomas Reid (1710–1796), Douglas Steward (1753–1828), William Hamilton (1788–1856), etc.—something analogous to our conclusion. Jacques Chevalier summarizes it in this way: the relativity of human knowledge "refers us back to an Absolute, because this Absolute is perceptible precisely in the gap that exists between knowing subject and object to be known" (*Histoire de la pensée*, tome IV [Paris: Flammarion, 1966], 337–38). One might say: every real object is an objection; the supreme objection reveals the supreme Object. But God is not "only" an Object.

6. See Jean Borella, *The Crisis of Religious Symbolism*, 358–72.

7. *Pensée* 225, in *Pascal's Penseés*, 63.

8. On Evagrius of Pontus, cf. *Amour et Vérité*, 342–52.

The Sense of "God" Dwells in Every Man

Surely this operation of conceptual stripping-away can be compared to what is now called "deconstruction." And, in fact, we must admit that there is, in our thought of God, a great deal of the "constructed": how could it be otherwise? But—and this is a major question—in whose name is this deconstruction carried out? For the unbeliever, it is in the very name of the "constructed" character of the idea of God, an idea which, once its constitutive elements are "disassembled," would reveal its inanity. However, this work of deconstruction tells us nothing about the very fact of construction: why was this idea constructed in the first place? In reality, deconstructivism presupposes the idea of God as the synthetic principle presiding over the making of this idea, which is contradictory, "God" being seen both as producing principle and produced result.[9]

We find a similar approach with the believer, insofar as his faith leads him to strip away from the idea of God in himself everything we have added to it, but with this difference: the idea of God is a real idea (and not a pseudo-idea as maintained by atheism), and it is in the name of this idea's truth alone that we can accomplish within ourselves the stripping-away of everything that is not this truth, if only we decide to take the path of this stripping-away, which is that of "negative" theology, a path whose obligations cannot be imposed on all minds.

Moreover, not only does "affirmative" theology remain true for all who believe in God, but it is equally necessary for those few who, by vocation, follow the path of negative theology: no one, save for the rare exception, is able to live his faith for length of days solely at the level of infinite ignorance. Still, it is necessary to distinguish here

---

9. Actually, to deconstruct the idea of God, one must first have this idea and analyze its components before subjecting them to a critique. The components do not therefore precede the idea, the cause of which they are claimed to be. They themselves are only the effect of an analysis of the cause they are supposed to produce. The idea of God is necessarily first, as Descartes shows in his Third Meditation on first philosophy: "the notion I have of the infinite is in me before that of the finite" (*The Philosophical Writings of Descartes: The Correspondence*, vol. 3, trans. by J. Cottingham, R. Stoothoff, D. Murdoch, and A. Kenny [Cambridge: Cambridge University Press, 1991], 377).

between the case of true mysticism, about which this essay does not pretend to speak, and that of the speculative mysticism, we venture to say, of the philosopher, the point of view we are considering here, and which in a certain way and at least in principle, if not in fact, concerns every believer. And yet again the question arises: how can we express the imperative to strip away our false knowledge of God, our false ideas about God, about Whom we say that we can have no adequate idea, except in the name and by the grace of a certain "idea" of the Divine Being? This "idea," this sense of God, must indeed be present in the depths of our minds, a presence revealed only negatively, as to the order of pure intellectuality, under the form of what we call an insurmountable transcendence. Infinite ignorance does not deconstruct the idea of God by dispersing it into the insignificance of its component parts without being able to leave behind its analytic functioning, indefinitely trapped in its vicious and repetitive circles, hopelessly "amiss from the Real," like a traveler who looks on helplessly from the window of a train as the countryside fleets past and is gone.

By stripping away false knowledge, faith's ignorance *obeys* a demand within itself, a demand that calls out to it and moves it, and of which it can never lay hold. Faith's ignorance obeys a higher and irrefutable *Reason*, a demand both unconstructible and more real than all the experiences it can have of the reality of things and beings, or rather by which it knows that within it all reality is fulfilled.

This innate sense of God dwells in every human soul, that sense of God by which we *know* that He surpasses all knowledge. This ignorance that is known is what Nicolas of Cusa calls "learned ignorance," ignorance that knows itself. It dwells in everyone, but is today unknown, suffocated, asphyxiated, massacred under the onslaught of a hatred of God such as the world has never seen. This hatred is suicidal, because by it we can attack God only *in ourselves*. It is not God whom we have killed or whom we would like to put to death; it is man himself, by sealing up in his heart the source by which his life is watered, by forbidding him to remember it, by binding him to his finiteness and inescapable, death-dealing contingency.

The Witness of Modern Painting

Some will suppose that these remarks are only due to the sentimentality of an aggrieved and nostalgic mind. Perhaps. But they also reflect the exact situation of our present civilization.[10] Two examples will show us, one borrowed from the history of contemporary painting, the other from the political world.

Of all the arts, painting is the one that makes us the most objectively present to the reality of the *world*, because it is, preeminently, the art of sight, the sense that reveals the world to us as a world, that is, as the fontal and unbounded space in which all things and all beings can appear and present themselves to us. Painting is open, while writing closes the objects of the world in upon themselves, in upon their mystery, and isolates them. If, then, there is an art expressing and disclosing the vision of the world that man bears within himself, more than any other, this art is painting. However, in modern and contemporary painting, the course of which is illustrated in exemplary fashion by Picasso and, even more, by Marcel Duchamp, along with Impressionism, Cubism, Surrealism and even the raw art of Dubuffet, the self-same unease *before* the real is expressed according to very diverse modes. The incredible reduction of the seen object to what Duchamp called "retinal painting," that is, to its purely sensory appearance, is a more-or-less conscious symptom of an amputation of our gaze upon the world: something is missing here. The painter clearly feels, deep inside himself, that the true reality of things, whatever it may be, and whatever idea we might have of it, cannot consist solely in their phenomenality. He knows it and he feels it as an amputee perceives his phantom limb, and he tries to make us understand it by superimposing on the "ret-

---

10. In *Ce que je crois* (Paris: Grasset, 1977), the great art historian René Huyghe shows that, from "Impressionism" to Vasarely, modern painting reveals its distress in the face of reality, as well as its fascination with the void, and betrays the *exhaustion of materialism*; a book read too late for us to take his remarkable analyses into account.

inal"[11] reality a certain deconstruction of this reality, a phantom substitute for the true, no-longer-perceived reality. This amputation, which has changed our sense of reality, is the result of many centuries of a triumphant scientism that has focused our consciousness of reality upon the materiality of its physical form. How could a real artist—Duchamp, Dubuffet, Picasso or many others—adopt this scientistic ontology? Why did medieval artists and those of all traditional civilizations, to use the language of Guénon, not experience this unease before reality?

We will start with the principle that the "desire for art," the will to create a work of art, can only spring from the feeling that the reality of the world needs to be *told*, needs to be shown. Why, then, this need? Why should the reality of the world need to be told? Is not simple sensory apprehension enough to inform us of this reality? Yes and no: yes, if we continually grasp that the visible mode of the real as perceived is sensory witness to the invisible form that dwells within it, is its basis and exceeds it; no, if we no longer perceive this presence and spontaneously reduce the real to its appearances, to its pure phenomenality, a "retinal" reduction that happens almost inevitably (and unconsciously) in the immediacy of daily life. Now, the artist is the one who strongly feels the need to speak the world, to speak it to men and to himself surely, but, more radically, to make this invisible form exist—as much as possible—in the human order through visible *works*. This is an exclusively human task: to accomplish it is to fulfill the primary function of the human being.

Ars homo additus naturae, "art is man added to nature"; but this could also be translated: "man is art added to nature." Man, that is to say (with regard to the arts of the beautiful) the consciousness of the invisible, man as that being of the world in which the world gains access to the knowledge of its spiritual and metaphysical reality, to this "soul supplement" spoken of by Bergson.

---

11. "Retinal," yes, because the appeal of modern painting lies at least as much in the *distancing* presented by the painting from the common and "realistic" appearance of its motif as in the pictorial virtuosity of its execution. This proves that the realistic or, if one prefers, "retinal" form of the object, by its very absence or deformity, is always present in the painting.

Now, this process of showing forth invisible reality, a mission accepted by the artist, can be done in many ways. To be brief, we will distinguish two. According to the first way, for the undeniable reason that our initial knowledge of the real is that communicated to us by our sensory apprehension of things, the artist will make this spiritual and invisible reality perceptible in the very showing-forth of its visible and corporeal presence: here no unease before the sensible world, no deformation of things, but on the contrary, the most attentive fidelity to their natural presence, to their integral presence (not to the photographic reduction thereof), an attention that allows the world to speak. The invisible reality, to whomever knows how to see, is not hidden by the bodily modality of its presence; it does not have to be superadded or superimposed on the perceived form, but it shows itself directly in the body itself, just as nature presents it to us: appearance is transparency. And how could there be a form more adequately transparent than that of its appearance, since it was God who willed it to be *thus* and not otherwise? Art is not meant to invent this theophanic presence, but only to make it visible, to let it appear as much as it can without belying the formal word with which God has endowed it. This is what we have called, in an expression borrowed from Novalis, "magical realism," which, in modern painting, Maurice Denis and Augustin Renouart have known how to illustrate so admirably.

According to the second way—and this is the path much of modern painting has taken—the artist who strongly feels the indigence of the "retinal" reduction of reality strives to remedy this by disfiguring the appearance, even torturing it, forcing it to say what it can no longer say for itself, because his gaze has lost the spiritual sense of the visible. In truth, there is no retinal *reduction* of the visible, it is not the eye that is misled; it is the intelligence and the consciousness of those who, in three or four centuries of atheistic scientism, have gradually been conditioned to reject the innate sense of the divine and the sacred, which nevertheless remains in the depths of all human thought, as evidenced by the enchanted perception of children of the world's sensory presence, the memory of which remains in us as a miraculous event. Subject in this way to a kind of materialistic oath, modern culture suffers in its metaphysical soul, a soul that it is constantly called upon to deny. Modern painting is the irrefutable witness to this suffering.

The Era of Dead Ideologies,
or the Dictatorship of the Nothing[12]

We come now to the second piece of evidence we would like to bring forward. It is less surprising than the last, but it is also, in many ways, much more serious and far more laden with consequences. It is this lack of a reason for living which today, in the opinion of the best observers, marks all the most powerful societies, such as the Chinese and American, both of which have entered the era of posthumous or even "ghost" ideologies, akin to the pictorial ghosts that haunt modern painting: post-Marxism for China, post-capitalism for the United States. This is consistent with the logic of history, since Marxism and capitalism, both by-products of scientist materialism, are the two dominant ideologies. Ghost ideologies, yes, because those who are their political and cultural agents have ceased to believe in them, but, for the moment, continue to impose them officially or promote them. The reality is a desert of social ideals. Wherever it has gone, and especially where it has been or is still politically instituted, Marxism has destroyed all inheritance from the past (let us make a clean sweep of the past) and replaced it with nothing. This is particularly the case in some African states where all the popular traditions—those that have given life to Africa for millennia—have disappeared under the most deadly and senseless dictatorships, like those in Russia, China, or Cambodia, all of them triumphs of collective *paranoia*. Yet Russia has escaped ideological desertification thanks to the presence of the Orthodox Church, which Stalinism did not succeed in defeating; a Church too "Russian" for some Catholic observers who seem to ignore that a people

---

12. The word *ideology* can be used in two different although related senses: either, to designate it in a neutral manner, the sum total or the system of philosophical and religious ideas as well as the cultural representations of a society; or, pejoratively, to characterize any doctrine that has no concern for reality. The *ideological* desert about which we are speaking here designates then, in the first sense, the state of a society that has lost every religious, philosophical, or general cultural ideal.

does not only live by political and institutional principles, but first of all by a faith in the reality of its religious soul. In some ways, the drama of Marxism is metaphysical and has a bearing on the cultural sphere. That of capitalism is physical and has a bearing on the material sphere. It does not *doctrinally* eliminate the religious and metaphysical soul of humanity, it eliminates it *in practice*. It does not essentially attack ideas, it ignores them and makes them useless: it proves, *de facto*, that they are useless. Having attacked the doctrinal theses of traditional culture, collapsing Marxism makes visible the ideological desert to which it has led. On the contrary, capitalism, by simply ignoring these metaphysical ideals by the sole and very apparent manifestation of its material success, masks the ideological desertification, a desertification it provokes, not as its primary and desired objective, but as its secondary and inescapable effect. This is why its success lasts longer than that of Marxism: it produces a real *anesthesia* of the ideological consciousness, an anesthesia which is that of the West's present humanity.

No doubt this consciousness seems to wake up when it appears that an ideologically inspired aggression physically threatens its political institutions, its social behaviors, even its media productions. We then invoke the rules of democracy, the immortal values of our civilization. And yet this ideological awakening, however justified and sincere, betrays most often a lack of knowledge and, even more, a deep misunderstanding of what is at stake. When we speak of fanaticism or barbarism, we believe we have said everything, but the horror of the accusation makes us forget what is the root of the evil. Fanaticism or barbarism, whether of a religious or political nature (as in the case of National Socialism), is rooted in a faith. Now, scientistic materialism, which is well illustrated by the positivist and self-satisfied mentality of Monsieur Homais,[13] has completely alienated us from any spirit of faith. In the true sense of the term, modern thought quite simply no longer *knows* what this is all about, hence its confusion when confronted with the most extreme and frenzied manifestations of this faith. In an emergency, modern thought counters this situation with its own "values," which, under

---

13. An emblematic character in Gustave Flaubert's *Madame Bovary* (1857).

the effect of these ideological aggressions, recover a kind of life. Thus, in a study of political philosophy devoted to the celebration of the Declaration of the Rights of Man and of the Citizen of 1789, Valentine Zuber concludes that "republican values" were "miraculously re-enchanted, thanks to the appearance of a new enemy to outwit, Islam."[14] But the call to "values" is itself only a shameful alibi for what were once straightforwardly called basic principles and truths, notions now rejected because they refer to being and "smack" of metaphysics. What should counter these manifestations of a faith become insane is another faith, a spontaneous and living recognition of a divine transcendence, a sense of God not only present in the human heart—awakened in us by all religious education—but connatural with every understanding and friend to all knowledge.

An Understanding in Faith

Still, we must be clear: when we suggest countering delusional manifestations of faith with an understanding of faith that is, in its intellectual depths, a true sense of the supernatural, we are not claiming to wage a victorious war on the enemy. This is not a religious war, and this book is not addressed to possible confederates in a warlike ideology. We are addressing the Western reader, and it is he who must be warned about the risk of a "dementia" of faith. Now this requires that the dementia be recognized at its root for what it is, namely, a deviation from what is known in its forthright truth by the intellect. Otherwise, deviant faith may impose itself by its very deviance, since the Western intellect, no longer understanding the language of faith, no longer has anything to say, anything specifically concerned with faith. It is sometimes surprising that young Europeans, educated in the West, succumb to a fascination with extreme ideologies, while their minds have been carefully rid of the darkness of religious superstition and belief in God: atheism—proven by science—now that is normalcy! But this "conversion" is

14. *Le culte des droits de l'homme* (Paris: Gallimard, 2014), 365; cf. J.G. Boher, "Au spectacle des droits de l'homme," in *Catholica* 126 (2015): 128–31.

on the contrary almost unavoidable. For "man does not live by bread alone" (Matt. 4:4), and the hunger for the spiritual and the transcendent is not the artificial product of a bad, alienated and alienating education; it is embedded in the nature of our spirit, which innately aspires to some absolute. When this thirst for the absolute no longer has a speculative *object* with which to invest itself, an absolute objectively known and thought of as a transcendent, then it subjectively invests itself in an "absolute" act and lives it as such; there is nothing but killing or giving oneself over to death.[15] On the other hand, intellective faith, which is known as intellection; that is, as intentional, as an orientation towards an *object* that by definition eludes it ("Glory of long desire, Ideas"),[16] this faith "situates" the desiring subject in its *relation* to object-being, to absolute being, and therefore situates it in its *relativity*. He thus learns that no act of the human subject can gain access to absoluteness, and therefore cannot reunite with absoluteness, even after "serving" it: "we are unprofitable servants" (Luke 17:10).

Surely it will be objected: even though the intellective nature of faith (faith is an "act of the intellect," says St. Thomas Aquinas) can preserve faith from the deviations of activism, this is not enough to preserve it from speculative aberrations. It is only too obvious that one can intellectually subscribe to all kinds of ideologies. Even if one admits, as one should, that reason and common sense are an indispensable aid here, the fact remains that, given the intervention of an indefinite variation of viewpoints, any ideological option is ultimately justifiable. That is why access to *true faith* is a grace, and faith, true faith, can logically only be a gift of heaven, as Catholic doctrine teaches. This implies that, strictly speaking, the true faith is not humanly justifiable. We have so far considered faith as a

---

15. A hypothesis about Louis Althusser's killing of his wife in a fit of madness: could he have been obsessed with the desire to *finally* perform a real—because definitive—act and so escape the maddening imprisonment in the "yes-and-no" to which his abandonment of Marxist scientism had condemned him, Marxism whose dogmatism he had embraced so avidly at first, following his loss of Christian faith?

16. Stephen Mallarmé, "Prose pour des Esseintes," in *Mallarmé*, trans. A. Hartley (Baltimore, MD: Penguin Books, 1965), 63.

movement of the human being towards the object of his adherence, in short as going from Earth to Heaven. But this movement must itself be seen—not psychologically, because we are not aware of it, but ontologically—as the human response to a mysteriously heard call of God, by which He offers us His love and His life. This amounts to saying that all philosophical discourse stops here with this response. It can indeed be shown—and we have tried to do so—that intelligence is ordered in its depths to the thought of God, so that, when it commits itself in faith, that is, when it commits the human being as a whole in an adherence to the reality of the Divine Being known in its thought, the intelligence obeys logically and with complete conviction the truth of what it thinks.

All of this is conceivable as long as it is about faith "in general," about the concept of faith, and, as philosophers, we have intentionally kept ourselves on this level. But to be committed in faith is to commit to a *particular* faith, not faith in general, which is a mere concept. With the commitment of faith we enter into the existential order, no longer a commitment to a faith imagined but to a faith lived in a personal relationship; no longer faith as such, but such or such a faith. But how do we decide *a priori*, among all the forms of faith that history offers us, the one that is true? Or what is the divine will for me? Surely, there are all kinds of arguments that can be made in favor of a particular form: this is called apologetics, which has its role to play. But, assuming that such a choice is possible—in reality an untenable supposition—it follows that human logic would determine the divine logic and render the work of grace superfluous. That is why philosophy has nothing to say here. That is why it is necessary to admit that faith is first and foremost a gift of God and that the first—and properly radical—reason for our commitment to a given faith, or, to put it more simply, the reason for our belonging to a given religion, eludes us. And this elusiveness is, in truth, a grace.

Conclusion

The point of this brief essay was not a denunciation of science, which would be even more ridiculous than vain. Science, insofar as it is knowledge of the truth, is a work worthy of admiration; the philosopher as much as the theologian is sure of this, and there is no need to convince anyone. But what we have denounced, as strongly as possible, is the incredible claim of a materialistic scientism, which believes it can draw from science proof of atheism. A thorough treatment of this question would have required much more extensive analysis, both in terms of the scientific approach and in terms of its results. This was not our intention, and, besides, there is no shortage of works that are engaged in it. We only wanted to emphasize that by taking this path materialistic scientism has betrayed both the truth of science and the dignity of the intelligence.